A WAR OF WITCHES

A WAR OF WITCHES

A Journey into the Underworld of the Contemporary Aztecs

TIMOTHY J. KNAB

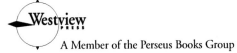

A Member of the Perseus Books Group

Grateful acknowledgment for permission to excerpt material from *A Scattering of Jades* by T. J. Knab and Rita Wilensky. Translations from Nahautl copyright © 1993 by Rita Wilensky. Original material copyright © 1993 by T. J. Knab. Reprinted by permission of Simon & Schuster, Inc. Chapter illustration based on a Teotihuacan flower design motif courtesy of Doris Heyden. Illustration by Jaime Robles.

First published by HarperCollins in 1995.

Library of Congress Cataloging-in-Publication Data
Knab, T. J.
  A war of witches: a journey into the underworld of the contemporary Aztecs / Timothy J. Knab. — 1 st ed.
      p.   cm.
  ISBN 0-06-251264-1 (hc)   ISBN 0-8133-3387-3 (pbk)
  1. Nahuas—Magic. 2. Nahuas—Religion. 3. Nahuas—Rites and ceremonies. 4. Witchcraft—Mexico—Puebla. 5. Shamanism—Mexico—Puebla. 6. Rites and ceremonies—Mexico—Puebla. 7. Puebla (Mexico)—Social life and customs. 1. Title

  F1221.N3K53 1995
  133.4'3'097248—dc20   94-41813

                        10 9 8 7 6
This edition is printed on acid-free paper that meets the American National Standards Institute Z39.48 Standard.

For the white-haired woman who insisted I embrace
her tradition,

Miek tasocomatic tonantzin

CONTENTS

Chapter 1

DISCOVERIES

September 12, 1974, San Martín Zinacapan,
Sierra de Puebla, Mexico

A WOMAN
WITH A RED POLYETHYLENE
RAIN SHAWL PICKED HER WAY
through the mud-clouded rivulets
and puddles
along the rutted path to the house of Don Inocente.

I had been sitting inside with the old gentleman most of the morning while he helped me translate a tape of one of his fantastic stories I had made several days before. Don Inocente was a master narrator, an accomplished teller of tales. This slight, white-haired old man could talk with a dozen voices, whispering and shouting, his words rumbling and rolling from what seemed like the depths of his being.

From where I was seated I could see through the open door that the woman with the rain shawl was headed toward us. It had been raining quite hard so we had had no visitors to interfere with our work. Though it almost always rains in the afternoons in that part of the Sierra de Puebla, the sun had now turned the entire landscape into bright yellows and greens.

The woman would definitely halt our work on Don Inocente's tale. I was not pleased.

She had been to market, judging by the full basket under her shawl, and probably mass, judging by her clothing. She must have been from San Andrés, a nearby village; beneath the rain shawl, I could see that the red-and-black handwoven belt that held her voluminous black wool skirts was the design used only in that town. As was usual in this part of the Sierra, she was wearing over her head her best *quechquemitl,* a triangular garment of pre-Columbian origin. It was made from a fine, white gauze-weave lace she had probably loomed herself. Underneath this, her head was piled high with her *mecapal,* a crown made of heavy strands of dark purple and deep green wool intertwined with strands of the hair of her ancestors. Knotted and wound around the top of her hair, it made a great tiara more than a foot high.

Her husband and children may have still been in Quetzalan, or perhaps the *niños* were on their way home, also loaded with the week's provisions, while Papa stayed in town for a few belts of *refino,* a fiery local cane alcohol. Dressed like this, she was definitely not in San Martín to gossip with other women about the neighbors or the guava crop just starting to come in—this she could do on any day. She had come to Don Inocente's door with a purpose.

"My dearest old uncle, my honored *compadre,* our honored little father, is the day darkening?" she called out in a lilting and deferential manner as she came up to the door. Nahuat is closely related to Classic Aztec and is most probably the language of the ancient Toltecs. Because it was on the outskirts of the old empire, the Sierra de Puebla has a dialect that does not use honorific words as much as other forms of Modern Aztec, but the proper use of words is still highly valued. Even here, leaders are called *tatoani*—"the speaker," "master of the word," "the one who says something." This woman was using the most elegant forms of the language that she could muster, so determined was she to see Inocente. Her visit would seriously interfere with our work, but there was nothing I could do about it.

Don Inocente got up from where he was seated on the low bench in front of his family altar, which dominated the main room of the hut. Running his hand through his white hair and feeling his way along the table in front of me where I had my notes and tape recorder, he made his way to the door. There he stood, as if trying to look out at the woman. His feeble eyes were so clouded, though, that he could perceive little beyond bright light and darkness.

"Enter my poor house, my little daughter," he answered, but with not nearly the refinement of the woman who had come visiting.

The woman came inside. I got up from the table next to the wall, and Inocente made his way back to his seat in front of the altar. I ducked my head under the lantern hanging from the smoke-darkened ceiling and looked down at the two of them. There would probably be no more translating done that afternoon.

Stepping outside, I sat on a low bench under the eaves with just a flimsy wall made of old boards between them and me. I lit up a cigarette and looked out at the street. There were chickens next to a pig rooting around in the neighbor's yard, an emaciated yellow dog with festering sores scratching itself, and two children playing in the muddy puddles. In the other direction, toward Quetzalan, the semitropical hills to the west were studded with coffee bushes under a canopy of tall trees. The bright red berries would be ripe in a few months. The sun was out in full now, making the whites and grays of the clouds blossom into a puffy elegance.

Don Inocente had been introduced to me as a healer, bone setter, and professional raconteur. He and Doña Rubia, a charming old sorceress, had taken it upon themselves to tutor me in the ways of the villagers. Like other people in San Martín, Don Inocente was under the impression that I did not speak much Nahuat, and that therefore it was safe to talk about whatever they pleased in my presence. However, in the course of my studies at the National School of Anthropology and History in Mexico City, and while living in Cholula near the city of Puebla, I had learned two related dialects of Aztec, so I could follow, in a rough way, what was said in Nahuat. I was learning more this way, and it set the people at ease when they were around me. My tape recorder was still on, so I sat and smoked, looked out at the hills, and listened to what I could of the conversation.

I wondered why the woman, so elaborately dressed, wanted to see Inocente. Inocente was a well-known practitioner of the traditional healing arts, so she was probably just another client. The old man had a flourishing practice, and we were always being interrupted. Some patients Inocente would treat immediately by feeling their pulses and massaging them in various places and prescribing an assortment of herbal teas. Some he would pray for and make offerings for at his altar; he would "do what he could for them." Others would be told to return on another day. I was hoping that this woman would be one of those told to come back so that we could get on with our translation. I listened intently to their conversation through the thin wall.

"Yes, my good woman, what is it that thou shouldst seek in my house?" Inocente said.

"O that I could tell you, O sir, all of the things that have befallen my humble house," the woman began. "You, sir, who see so clearly," and I imagined her looking into the cataracts that covered his eyes, "you must see what has befallen me and my children, my humble house. O please, sir."

"My good woman," the old man asked, "are you perhaps the daughter of my honored *compadre,* José?" He was still using the formal manner of *compadres,* ritual kinsmen. These are people bound even closer than kinship by mutual social obligations, and he was obviously trying to place her. The old man's gray eyes couldn't see the belt that indicated she was from San Andrés, but he must have known by her accent she was not a Sanmartino.

Quickly she explained that he had been recommended to her by a distant mutual relative for whom Inocente had once done some favors. She was in fact not a *compadre* at all, yet she continued to use the archaic manner of speech to show the old man the greatest respect possible.

"My good woman, what could have possibly befallen your humble house to cause you to come all the way here to see this little old man?" he asked. By this time Inocente probably knew exactly why she was there, and what she wanted as well, but he had obviously decided to hear her tale before getting down to business. He asked her what her problem was.

"It is my . . . my . . . daughter," she said haltingly, and in a very circuitous way she began to explain.

Her daughter had just run off with a young man from the indigenous section of the town of Quetzalan, and for all intents and purposes, by local tradition, they were man and wife. Now the boy was working as a mason in the far-off city of Puebla, the state capital. The mother and her husband had been trying to arrange a proper marriage for their daughter in their own village. This was truly a tragedy, as she explained, for they thought that they had found a hard-working candidate who would help with the harvesting and planting. They needed this help and more with their coffee, she went on, but their ungrateful daughter had cheated them by running off. Now, they had nothing.

What was worse, the woman continued, was that the young man who had stolen their daughter had taken some of their chickens and a small amount of money from the house when he eloped with her. Of course, their daughter could have had nothing to do with this, she assured Inocente.

I thought it very likely that the daughter, hearing of an unwanted match that had been arranged by her parents, had taken more than a small part in the scheme. The loss of their daughter represented a serious economic blow to the family, as a son-in-law usually spends at least a year helping his wife's parents before setting up his own household or returning with his wife to his own parents' home. In some cases a daughter's husband may even opt to stay with his in-laws permanently, which gives them a huge advantage in labor.

The elopement, I surmised, was not at all spontaneous, for the young couple would have had to purchase bus tickets several days in advance. As the woman told her story, I realized that I knew the young man slightly; he had been one of the masons working for the Secretary of Education's office on the new schoolhouse in San Andrés. I also knew that the architect in charge of the project had found him a job in Puebla, and that he had been down there for several months before the elopement. This was surely not the case of bride theft that the woman sitting in front of Inocente tried to make it seem, though this used to be a fairly common practice in the region. The conversation was starting to become interesting, and I was no longer sorry that our translation had been interrupted. I listened eagerly.

Upon the completion of her woeful tale, Inocente asked, "What, my good woman, would you wish to befall this young man?" Immediately she replied, "Something a bit bad, a bit evil, O sir." "Oh, you seek justice for this thing that has come to pass in your humble house?" said Inocente.

"Justice" is a very important point for someone seeking the help of the Lords of darkness. If "they" see that one's cause is just, they can wreak havoc among the living—with some help from a witch or sorcerer, of course. I had heard of the "evil eye of envy" and the "night winds," but in my training I had been led to believe that witchcraft in the Sierra de Puebla was little more than sympathetic magic. I thought its effectiveness was based simply on the strong shared beliefs of client, practitioner, and victim. If everyone believed it would work, it worked. If the sorcerer had any direct role, it was through a well-placed whispering campaign or malicious gossip or through letting others know that the victim had been "witched."

The old man began to explain the things he could arrange that were "a bit bad." On the one hand, it sounded like the standard repertoire that I had heard before in the classroom and in the field. On the other hand, previous researchers had remarked that because of a number of killings in the 1920s and '30s, San Martín had a rather sinister reputation as a town full of witches.

Even nonindigenous people in nearby Quetzalan thought of San Martín as a dangerous place. Though they paid little heed to tales of witchcraft—it was just something "those Indians" did to one another—it was still cause for comment. I thought of Doña Rubia, Inocente's *comadre*, and her harrowing tales of dreams in which she sought to salvage bewitched souls. In the five years I had been coming to the region, I had known at least two people who reportedly died of witchcraft. One woman, whom I took to Quetzalan to see the local pharmacist, "Doctor" Morán, seemed to have lost the will to live upon hearing she had been witched. The effect could have been due to sympathetic magic and suggestion, but what I was hearing now started to convince me there was more to it than I, or my colleagues, had guessed.

"The evil winds that carry the 'shadow of death' generally go from north to south. Because Puebla is in the south, perhaps one of these could strike him so that your daughter would return to her house. This, though, is fraught with danger, for the evil winds are not easily directed. They may pierce her heart, too, for when the 'shadow of death' descends it may strike anyone. When the winds blow from the caves of the bats, they blow everywhere and strike anyone," Inocente cautioned.

With mounting excitement, I strained to hear what was being said.

"The 'shadow of death,'" the old man went on, "will take his dark shadow, his *ecahuil*, down deep. It will kill his *nagual* and surely the *tonal*, his soul, will follow it into the underworld. Then he is as good as dead, but for that I must see his 'true' shadow first, if I am to take it. We could also place the 'flower of darkness' somewhere on him."

The "flower of darkness," I knew, was the metaphoric term used for the shape and form of the underworld, but in this case it turned out to be a small piece of a thick, black leaf. He assured her it was a *yohualxiuit*, "a leaf of darkness," and not a *hoja santa*, "a holy leaf." On the smooth side of the leaf, which is the surface that can be touched, a mixture of resin and clay was painted. On the other side, a small wad of ground obsidian was mixed with the plant poison and fixed with a glue made from the pseudobulb of a local orchid. This was covered over with another thin leaf and another coating of glue. Great care was to be used in handling this "flower," he explained to the woman. It should be "given" to the intended victim, perhaps with an embrace, or a pat on the back, and "planted" just below the nape of the neck, if possible. Even if the victim discovered it before the toxins took effect, he or she would know there was a witch around. At that point the power of suggestion and fear would become as potent as the "flower" itself. This last part was all that anthropologists had been able to learn about.

"There is also the 'night of death' that could befall him," Inocente went on. "This brings the darkness of the cave into his heart and soul, his *yollo* and *tonal,* and puts them in the underworld, Talocan. For this I must have something of him, some hair, or some fingernails, perhaps some of his clothing; the underwear is the best." ("Loincloth" was the archaic term he used in Nahuat.) "These things I will place in the night. Then, on his *petate,* his sleeping mat, you must leave the ash of these things I will burn with copal for the Lords. Then the darkness of the night, of the cave of the Lords, will enter his heart, and it will not be long before his heart remains there forever in the darkness of the earth. This, though, is dangerous, for if he sleeps with your daughter, it could take her, too, if they share the same mat."

Another subtle technique Inocente described involved dusting the young man's clothing with a powder made from resins of another local plant called jaguar's paw mixed with a finely ground clay. This would be extremely difficult to remove, causing severe skin irritation and open, festering sores, but as to whether it would be toxic enough to cause death, he was uncertain. He assured the woman, however, that it would cause the young man great suffering.

"This is like the 'flowers of death,' which someone also has to put in his sleeping room, but this would certainly get the both of them if it was when they were 'sharing the mat.'" He was making a sly sexual allusion. "The darkness of night would consume them then; it would get their souls and keep them together, forever."

In a slightly sinister tone, Inocente explained that the "flowers of death" is a powder produced from a deadly white flower ground and mixed with a fine, white limestone powder. When victims inhaled the dusty mixture, "they would not continue to walk the paths of this earth for long. They would rest forever."

"The 'evil eye' and the 'shadow of death' are two others, but I would have to go to Puebla if you wanted me to do them," he added. "Once this was done, though, their days together would not continue, and your daughter would have to return home. For the others, you could visit your daughter with the things I would give you; that would be enough to cut the young man's candle short, to let his life burn out.

"If it is truly justice that you seek, the Lords of the earth will grant that, if they are asked in the right way. The Most Holy Earth is just. If this young man has done all this with an evil heart, if he has truly stolen your daughter, your little one, then they will give us justice there in the earth. They will take him from us on the earth. Perhaps it is the 'night wind' that we should use to take care of this young man," Inocente concluded.

"And what is the 'night wind,' O sir?" the woman asked.

"Give your daughter some candles and incense that I will prepare for you. Tell her they are for him so that they will have a strong young son. That should bring his path to an end. She must have him burn them while she is out of the house. They will carry the 'night wind' to him. The 'night wind' is in the smoke. It is dense and black as the night. It comes from the 'night flower,' the *yohualxochit,* which, when it opens, lets the darkness of the cave come out into the world.

"I mix the juices of this night flower with the candles and some copal incense, and the smoke will never let him see the light of day again. It must be burned in a small room, maybe at their altar," Inocente suggested. "If you tell your daughter it is for a strong child, then maybe he will do this. Then we'll cut his thieving candle short!" The old man chuckled.

The plant of which Inocente spoke contains a powerful neurotoxin, and I realized that when burned in a closed room it could paralyze the lungs or at least make breathing very difficult. And I had always thought that the "night wind" was a benign metaphor that was part of sympathetic magic!

"That would be just," the woman replied and said that she was certain her daughter would accept the gift. After a few formal social pleasantries, the two of them got up and came to the door.

"That will be ten pesos, please," Inocente said, "and I will prepare it on my altar tonight. You must come back in five days." The woman reached inside her blouse, extracted a bill, and handed it to him.

I was leaning against the wall, still amazed at what I had heard but trying not to show it. Putting the money into his shirt pocket, Inocente nodded a final good-bye to the woman. Then he turned to me, smiled, and looked in my direction with his blind eyes. In Spanish he said, "Well, isn't it fortunate that there are only *curanderos* here? Isn't it fortunate there are no more witches?"

This delightful old man who had been so helpful to me during my stay in the village was not only a healer, he was capable of murder! He was my confidant in the village. With his friend Doña Rubia, a fellow *curandera,* he had been teaching me his language and how to behave as a proper Sanmartino. Now he was secretly laughing at me!

With a coy smile, Inocente went on, "Once, you know, there were many witches here. Oof! There were plenty of them, dozens of them, hundreds of them, everywhere around, and then they all killed one another off, as everyone knows. There once was a time when this town was renowned for its witches. They were all over everywhere, doing their evil work!"

As the woman walked away, he motioned me to come back inside. Coming in, I reached over the table and, as noiselessly as possible, turned the tape recorder off. On the other side of the table, Inocente felt his way back to his low stool in front of the altar. Reaching behind it, he took out a bottle of *yolixpa,* literally, "in the face of the heart," a powerful local herb liquor not unlike Chartreuse, and two small glasses.

"Well, you know it!" he said, as we sat down again. "This town had a lot of witches once, but they were all killed off by their own evil deeds. Here! Warm your heart and they won't darken your days." He poured out and handed me a small shot of the greenish liquor.

After pausing to pour himself one and take a sip, he continued to tell me about the evil things that witches once did in San Martín. He began to recount some memories of what he called *la guerra de los brujos,* "the War of Witches." They were fragments, but quite detailed, and even included a short list of the victims. My own feelings were fragments, too, but of anger and glee at what I was finding out. I wrote furiously. Don Inocente's face became animated as he talked about those days, and we had a few more drinks. He ended the discussion by affirming again that witchcraft was a thing of the past.

"It is lucky that all the witches are dead now, is it not? They were foul and evil, damned things. Evil things," he repeated, with finality.

THERE WERE TWO ways to get back to Quetzalan, where I was staying, and I chose the old cobblestone path through the jungle. My head began to clear, and I began wishing I had not heard that conversation correctly. Perhaps they had only been talking in metaphors. Perhaps this young man was not about to be murdered by his mother-in-law! But at least some of the things they had talked about would really work, that I knew. The "winds from the bat caves" that Inocente had mentioned made me think of two young archaeologists in Yucatán who had recently contracted the "bat disease." The bat disease was quite common in the Sierra, and several caves were reputed to harbor the spores responsible for it. All of them were well known as witches' caves. The archaeologists had both been misdiagnosed as having tuberculosis, and when it was finally discovered in Mexico City that this was the bat disease, it was too late for one of them. The other suffered permanent lung damage.

I was very anxious to listen to the tape again as soon as I returned to my hotel. When I got back to my room, I plugged in the recorder. I took care to put on the earphones lest someone overhear. The handyman and all the maids in the hotel spoke Nahuat, and Polo, the busboy, had even helped me with several translations. My Nahuat at that time was not as fluent as it would become, but it was sufficient to clearly understand, with the aid of my dictionary, most of the conversation. I still could not believe what I was hearing on the tape. I listened again, jotting down words and phrases I didn't know. I was at a loss what to do. I could not ask Inocente or any of the other *curanderos* about it. News travels fast in the Sierra, and this would be my last productive—if not, in fact, my last—trip up here if anyone found out what I had recorded. There was a Nahua schoolteacher in Mexico City, however, who had his own reasons not to return. I knew he would give me some help with the parts of the tape I still didn't understand.

After three or four listenings, however, what I could understand was becoming very eerie, complex, and convoluted. I thought of the young mason, a potential victim of "the justice of the underworld." Talocan was real to Inocente, and he was a facilitator of its powers. The "flower of darkness" was not a metaphor.

Of course I would warn the boy. I was saddened and troubled that something so serious could be taken so lightly. I would think of a way, of that I had no doubt, even if I had to use the schoolteacher or another friend of mine at the university.

I would have to be very careful, though. To think about the Aztec underworld as anything other than a vague and half-remembered notion mixed with misunderstandings of Catholicism would be considered heresy, or worse, by most of my colleagues in academia. This was because they had used only Spanish to interview the *curanderos*. *La santísima tierra*—"the sacred earth"—and *el infierno*—"the inferno"—were as concepts already half-Christianized in a translated language. Here, on the fringes of the old empire, the ancient religion of the Aztecs was still alive. It had not been eradicated by the Conquest.

I looked out into the darkness at the plaza across the street from where I was seated. I had read in the works of Fray Sahagún, a sixteenth-century Spanish priest:

> The witch, *naoalli,* the shape shifter, is a man of knowledge, a wise man, a possessor of all. . . .
> The good witch is a guardian, a keeper of the heart, a possessor of men. . . .
> The evil witch does foul things, makes things evil, shifts the shapes of words. . . .

What did it mean if the witch was also a healer? I had seen Inocente, Rubia, and the other *curanderos* perform some marvelous curings in my five years of coming up to the Sierra. Did what I had overheard mean that in invoking the "justice of the underworld," witches were still curing the ills of the earth, their mother and father, by murder?

Finally, near dawn, I fell asleep.

Chapter 2

THE CAVE

Two years later. July 10, 1976,
Sierra de Puebla, Mexico

QUETZALAN
IS AT THE END
OF A PAVED MOUNTAIN ROAD.
The great stone cathedral
that dominates the white-stuccoed town
is being eaten away.

The jungle has been trying to reclaim the church since it was built. Nascent trees sprout from the great tower, and moist airs give rise to black fungi and lichens that, from a distance, make the cathedral look like an ornament on an abandoned wedding cake. The town lies above the eastern coastal plains of Veracruz on the edge of coffee country, where the mountains rise to Mexico's central highlands. Here is a world almost lost and forgotten in the fogs of the cloud forests, where ferns grow larger than houses and fence posts sprout into trees. In the rainy season it is hot and vaporous, and the overgrown verdure always drips with moisture.

As reflected in the layout of its grandiose gardens, parks, and band shells, the town was a center of commercial activity at the end of the last century, but time has taken a toll and other areas have risen to greater importance. Most of its once-grand houses are inhabited now only by a dwindling cadre of old men and women. The young seek their way elsewhere. Though the town still blossoms on market day, with the indigenous peoples of the region coming in to buy and sell what local products there are, the grandeur is gone, the coffee boom over.

I had been driving from Mexico City through most of the gray afternoon, and when I arrived, it was dark and raining. I came around the last twisting curve into town, my jeep vibrating over the cobblestone streets. On the sides of the mountains, white stucco and gray stone buildings with great overhanging eaves loomed over me. The steep streets that ran between them often became stairways. I followed the main road past the cathedral, with its massive tower reaching up into the darkness and clouds.

Like most others in the region, the town had originally been laid out on the model of the ancient Aztec cosmos. The central plaza in front of the church is divided into four parts, radiating from an *axis mundi* at its center. There, a great pole hewn from a single tree reaches sixty feet into the air and also pierces the center of the underworld below. For the feast of Saint Francis in early October, the *voladores*, flying dancers who fling themselves on ropes from the pole's spinning peak, perform their ancient ritual descent to earth. In every town in the Sierra this pattern is repeated—the sky, the four directions of the earth, and the underworld. In the outlying vicinities, various caves serve as entrances to individual underworlds for each town. They are linked to one great underworld that lies below all of this land.

I kept on driving through the town and the darkness to the dirt jeep trail at the other end that led to San Martín, farther up in the mountains. News had reached me through a *National Geographic* team working in the area that Doña Rubia, Inocente's *comadre*, was gravely ill, perhaps dying. Rubia had been my mentor and had taught me more about Nahuat and curing than even old Inocente. Judging from what I had learned of Inocente the afternoon I left my tape recorder on, and from the magazine crew's secondhand reports of Rubia's condition, I suspected foul play—witchcraft.

Rubia was kind and grandmotherly, an excellent cook and a well-known *curandera*. She journeyed regularly at night to Talocan, the underworld of her Aztec ancestors, to find cures for her clients' troubled souls. Perhaps she was also an occasional practitioner of witchcraft herself, but she had always been very evasive about these matters, assuring me that all the witches were long dead.

Unlike Inocente, with his polite nods to the Catholic church, Rubia was a devout believer in the powers of the saints and Jesucristo. She put great stock in the gospels, prayers, and rituals of the church and was an active participant in the local Catholic Action development group.

Rubia lived dichotomously, maintaining a traditional set of relationships to the world around her yet wearing Western clothing, unlike most of the women in San Martín. Underneath the modern cotton shifts from Quetzalan, she always had a traditional native blouse and *naguas,* the long skirts of her ancestors. Around her weathered neck she wore a black string of beads that marked her as a practitioner with powerful knowledge of the ancient ways. In San Martín, even dogs and children wear something red to ward off the evil eye. Rubia, though, never wore red. The evil eye was not something she feared.

I followed the rough, winding route through the Sierra thinking about her. I wondered why Inocente simply answered my questions, while Rubia would talk far into the night. What seemed to be just minute details of her beliefs would slowly reveal her vast knowledge of herbs, curing techniques, and the gods, along with her profound grasp of people's personalities and the social affairs of the village. Rubia enjoined me to learn all this along with the meanings inherent in her Nahuat prayers and dreamtime journeys. She also insisted that I accompany her when she went curing. Why the old woman had been so willing to share all this with me I didn't know.

The night rolled on, and after what seemed like a long time, but I knew really wasn't, I found my way into San Martín, driving down its one deserted, muddy main street. The rain was still coming down, and the only light came from candles in the late-night family stores, whose doors opened onto the street. The electricity was out, as usual. I parked my truck behind the church, avoiding torrents of water that cascaded from the broken drainpipes under the roof. Rubia lived in the third house above the church plaza. Under a leaky umbrella, I made my way across the plaza and up the hill to Doña Rubia's rather plain white-plastered house.

I stood before her front door, lit a damp cigarette, and spoke loudly in Aztec. My archaic and formal greeting, "The night is good. I seek the sun," was a request to let me come into the house.

The smoke of the tobacco was to keep away the *ajmotocnihuan,* "those who are not our brothers," the mischievous supernaturals of the underworld who might have accompanied me in the darkness. "May the coming light of the sun destroy the darkness," I called out. I could hear movement in the house, and I knew that Lupe, Doña Rubia's plump, middle-aged daughter-in-law, was slowly and cautiously beginning to unbar the door. Lupita, whose husband was away teaching in Aguascalientes, cared for the old sage by keeping house and cooking. She had not expected anyone to come calling, especially at this hour of the night; it was rare that people in San Martín went out so late, for the world of darkness was always hungry for new souls.

"I am here to see our grandmother," I said, as she opened the door. Rubia was known in the town as everyone's grandmother.

As I was speaking, I could hear Rubia's faint voice from the kitchen asking what the matter was. At first Lupe looked rather astonished. She obviously did not expect a white-faced, bearded, six-foot apparition at the door. Like most of the villagers, she was barely five feet tall. As I began to speak, however, apologizing for arriving in the danger of night and the time of the underworld, recognition crossed her face.

"Open the door and let him in. It's the 'tree man,'" I heard Rubia say from the back. Many in the town knew me by that name, both for my habit of climbing tall trees in search of rare plants and orchids and for my height. "Light a candle and put the fire on for some coffee," she commanded weakly.

We walked into the kitchen, where Lupe began to start the fire with a bit of fresh tinder. Rubia was lying on a pallet in the back of the kitchen trying to prop herself up on an emaciated arm. Her deeply weathered face was pale, framing coal black eyes. Her snow white hair, always neatly braided, was now disheveled and hung about her shoulders. A bony hand reached out to me in greeting.

She was obviously quite sick. After I greeted Rubia again, she managed to struggle into a sitting position. She asked me about Mexico City, and I asked her about the village. The smell of sickness was overwhelming, and her breath came in short wheezes. Finally I asked, "What did Arturo recommend?"

Arturo was a doctor in Quetzalan who sometimes had worked with Rubia and who I knew was treating her. Rubia, besides being a devout practitioner of traditional curing, had great faith in Western medicine. She regularly recommended that her clients consult members of the local medical profession, and they, in turn, would sometimes refer their patients to her.

She showed me the medications she had been given, but most of them were unopened and unused.

"What about Don Inocente?" I asked. "What does he think?"

"It is the witches. That's what he thinks. Says there is nothing he can do."

I asked whether she thought she could find the cause of the illness herself, in her dreams. Over the past two years I had listened to many of her dream tales of epic battles in the underworld, where she had wrested the lost souls of her clients from the Lords of darkness. Now this was a new twist.

"Well, can't do much about those witches myself," she said. "They're simply too strong, and I'm too weak now."

Rubia alone could not find her soul in the underworld of the ancestors. If it was a case of witchcraft, as Inocente maintained, the battle she would have to undertake with the witch to get back her soul would probably kill her. In her opinion, it was better to hope that the witch slipped up somewhere in his or her ministrations for aid from the Lords of darkness. If there was a mistake, the Lords would get that witch and Rubia's soul would be freed.

We talked a short while longer, but I could tell that the old woman was weary. Finally, I asked, "Grandmother, may I say some words of light before venturing out into the deepness of night?" I wanted to say a short prayer at her altar, both to find her lost soul and to protect my own as I ventured out into the night. My request obviously pleased her, and she asked Lupe to burn some copal at the altar for me and light the candles. I followed Lupe through the side door of the kitchen into the darkened main room of the house. On the altar table in the half-light of a small votive candle were some fresh white flowers in an old vase. Laid out nearby was a pack of strong, dark tobacco cigarettes called Alas, five little glasses filled with water, some still-fresh tortillas, and a small bowl of cooked beans and sauce. Every family altar in San Martín is a miniature cosmos. As Lupe lit the candles on the table, or earth, part of the altar, I could see up on the wall the pictures of relatives, acquaintances, and the virgins and saints who represented the sky. Some of them, such as San Guillermo of the Glass of Red Wine, were completely unknown to the church. Below the altar table was the region of the underworld. Here relics of the ancestors would have been buried: perhaps some pre-Columbian potsherds, bones, and black flakes of obsidian. In a trunk over these would be some hair and clothes of departed relatives.

I intoned a short prayer in Nahuat loud enough so that Rubia could hear me, and then with her weakened voice she called me once more into the kitchen. "Can you come b-b-back in the dawning of the night?" she asked. She meant tomorrow afternoon.

I assured her that, of course, I would—it was why I had driven all day from Mexico City. Then I turned to go out. It had stopped raining and it was quiet. The calls of the insects had not returned. I walked down to my jeep and drove back to Quetzalan for the night.

I thought I had seen enough to know what the matter was. Her emaciated frame, the wheezing when she tried to talk, the unnatural brightness in her eyes—I had seen this before with those two archaeology students from Mexico City, the ones who had contracted the bat disease.

THE FIRST THING I did the next morning was visit Arturo. His parents ran the Hotel Rivoli, the site of the old town baths in better days. It was next to the plaza and across the street from where I was staying at Las Garzas, once a private home and now the town's most "elegant" hostelry.

"Well, look who's here! How have you been? In Mexico City all this time?" He greeted me with a big *abrazo,* rather than just a handshake.

"Mama! Papa! Look who's here! The professor from Mexico City!" he called out. "What brings you back up here to the Sierra?" he asked as his parents came out of the kitchen where they were having breakfast.

"It's Rubia."

"Not too well, is she? Have you seen her yet?" Arturo asked.

Doña Elvira and Don Victor, his parents, had coffee and sweet rolls brought as we sat down to talk. They were as pleased to see me as he was. We talked about Mexico City and the university for a while, but then I asked, "How is the old woman, Arturo?"

He told me about Rubia's symptoms, his diagnosis of tuberculosis, and the course of treatment that he thought would be best, but admitted that he was perplexed, as the treatment did not appear to be working. I remembered all the unopened containers of medication Rubia had, but rather than tell Arturo that, I decided to relate to him what Rubia thought.

Last year I had used my developing knowledge of the local sorcerers' crafts to help Arturo treat two bewitched villagers; both cases turned out to be rather sophisticated poisonings. By recognizing this, he had been able to treat them successfully, so

Arturo trusted my judgment in these matters. We knew now that witchcraft was no trivial matter.

"Arturo, remember those two students I told you about last year, the ones diagnosed as having TB but by the time they found out what it was, it was too late for one of them and the other might as well have been dead? The ones with the bat disease?"

Arturo looked at me and recognition came over his face. "It's the glassy eyes," he said.

The bat disease comes from a mold that grows on the droppings of certain bats in certain caves. When the guano dries, the mold becomes airborne. Why some caves and bats are safe and others deadly, no one knows. Around San Martín there were a number of "witches' caves" I had learned about, but no one would ever go there unless they had a foul purpose. If Rubia had gone to those caves, which I doubted, she would have always been careful. It was unlikely that she had contracted the disease accidentally— someone had to have put it in her house. Arturo and I knew what had to be done. We also knew it wasn't going to be easy with someone like Rubia.

On the way to the pharmacy for the disinfectant I decided that adding a bit of modern chemistry would help make things easier, so along with the other things I needed, I asked Martín, the pharmacist, for a few crystals of pure iodine, which he gave me in a small brown vial. He also suggested that I borrow a sprayer from the National Antimalarial Commission offices at the edge of town. For years the commission had sprayed every dwelling in Mexico from the National Palace to the most humble indigenous hut, effectively eliminating the mosquito-borne dread throughout Mexico.

Once equipped, I went straight over to Doña Rubia's house. Rubia was sitting on the stone stoop in the sun when I arrived. Carefully, in terms she would understand, I explained to her what I had brought and what I wanted to do. With the medical tests I had brought from Mexico City, there was little problem with the correct diagnosis, but as expected, she objected vociferously to disinfection of the house. Rubia took this as reflecting poorly on Lupe's housekeeping skills, and she was not willing to admit that her house was not clean. When Lupe came back, I took her aside and explained to her what needed to be done.

"I've wanted to clear out all this old stuff for a long time," she said. "It's a good excuse for a real cleaning." Lupe had solved the problem.

As I told her what had to be removed from the house before I could disinfect it, I prepared a bit of nitrogen triiodide. Once we had cleared the house, I sprinkled a bit of the compound on the floor. Nitrogen triiodide is highly unstable and will explode under its own weight when dry. Before I began to spray the house with disinfectant, I asked Lupe for a broom and began to sweep the floor, to "help" her with the cleaning. The effects were spectacular!

The compound began to explode all over as I swept. Lupe was quite startled, and the neighbors came out from everywhere around. Throughout, Rubia sat passively on the stoop. As the explosions died down, I began to spray and disinfect the entire house. It seemed that half the town was looking on. By the time I finished, everyone was thoroughly convinced by my modern-day sorcery that the house had been fully exorcised—everyone except Rubia. She knew the ways of witches and had never seen such a thing in her eighty years.

"Do you think that they are gone? You think a witch does that? I've never seen them do that," she stated flatly, quite sure that her experience in the matter was definitive.

We helped her back into the house, but when we got inside, Rubia insisted on sitting down before her family altar in the front room instead of returning to her pallet in the kitchen. We brought everything back into the house quickly with the help of some neighbors, and Lupe went about straightening up, while I wiped off the surfaces that were still wet with disinfectant. The smell was overpowering, but it dissipated quickly. To complete the arrangements, Lupe brought in the white lilies that Rubia liked because they protected her from the north winds. As her daughter-in-law arranged them on the altar and lit the votive candle, Rubia suddenly started speaking in a distant voice.

"Do youuuu knoooow the wooords of the holy eaaarth?" Her voice sounded as if it were coming from another world. She drew out the words and let them hang on her lips.

I was startled. I replied that, of course, I knew how to pray as she herself had taught me over a long period. I knew how to make offerings to the Lords of the earth, as well as to the sky.

"Nooooo!" she insisted, still with that strange, distant voice. "How to really pray, pray at the cave, pray with your heart and your soul. You say only . . . the words. You know only my words! You say them just the way I say the prayers, but you do not really pray; there is no reason that you pray. You only follow me. You let 'them' have your words, but you don't give them your heart and your soul. They will not help you without your heart and your soul; it is their food and sustenance; it is the soul they want." She was admonishing me for my feeble attempts at imitating the way she and Inocente ministered to the underworld Lords.

"You've been to the cave before. You know how to bring 'them' gifts. You know how to pay them their due," she insisted, looking straight at me. "NOW! you have to give them a heart, a soul. You have to do it for me. You have to let them take you through their world of darkness. That is their food, the sustenance that they lack. I am weak and old. With all my prayers, they will not find my *nagual,* they will not return my *tonal* to me. I need your *yollo,* your soul, your *tonal.* This is their nourishment. You're going to have to go there to the cave for me. Find those witches if you can!"

I was stunned. How would I be able to do that? When Rubia went hunting for a witch, she did it through her dreams.

She saw my reaction. "We can get you all the things you will need there in the cave. You can go there tonight. You are going to have to offer them your heart, and your soul."

I thought of the rather grisly practices of her Aztec ancestors, ripping beating hearts out of living victims for the gods. Going to the cave and offering them a heart and a soul was not something I looked forward to.

What I'd agreed to do seemed impossible. But perhaps it wasn't. I had learned a great deal from the old woman. She had insisted several times before that I had to learn to cure, but I had demurred. It was something that required a system of beliefs I did not think I had. I was an anthropologist who studied things—I did not actually do them and believe in them. This was something that required a commitment to serve the world of the ancestors as well as its children, the present-day Sanmartinos. Could I make this commitment? I had no idea what was in store for me, but there was no choice but to go forward.

The list of offerings and other items I would need was rather extensive, but most of them were easily obtainable in the village. Rubia began by having Lupe break off a few sticks of *ocote,* fatwood, to use if I needed a fire or a torch, which she preferred to a flashlight.

"Take care not to fall asleep down there, or they will come out to eat you in that place. They are eaters of our flesh, and they are always hungry," she warned. "We need five cigars and five packs of Alas." Alas were her favorite brand of cigarette. "Then also one pack for you to smoke and one to leave with me. Lupe, gather five types of flowers and leaves from the garden in back," she instructed.

I went out and bought the cigarettes, candles, a packet of heavy, dark native tobacco, and a bottle of *aguardiente,* cane alcohol, from Don Pedro up the street. Lupe started to warm some tortillas and cook a little container of *atole,* a corn gruel laced with hot peppers and epazote, for me to take to the cave. The smell of the cooking corn began to fill the room. Rubia had a good supply of copal, aromatic pitch incense, already on hand, so I sat down with her at the table, and we began to roll the five cigars I would need to smoke through the night. Tobacco and incense were to smolder constantly for placation of and protection from the Dark Lords of the Most Holy Earth and possibly from the bat disease. As long as one had tobacco one was safe, or so I had been told.

"Now, there will be the five flowers, the five leaves, the five nice fat beans, and the five tortillas, plus the *atole* and enough *aguardiente,* if you don't help yourself to too much, to get those 'things' there in the cave sauced." We finished rolling up the cigars. Rubia was very careful in describing how to lay out these offerings and how to order the prayers that had to be said, both to beseech the Lords for their aid and to protect my own soul. The prayers would plead, threaten, and cajole the Lords of the earth while I prostrated myself before them.

I began to see that worshiping in the cave was an activity that could easily open me up in the village to charges of witchcraft.

Rubia sent her daughter-in-law out to negotiate for the last item we needed to take to the cave: a black hen. "You have got to have a messenger," she said. "They've got to have the heart. That is their food. If you don't have a messenger they just might take *your* heart. A black hen is what we need; a night bird is the right messenger."

The black hen proved more than a bit difficult to obtain. Chickens were now, in fact, rather rare in San Martín. Disease had wiped out most of the flocks about a year ago. Lupe came back with a young, mostly black, cock. No one would sell her a hen because they were much too valuable for their eggs. She carried it by its neatly tied legs and set it on the table, where it looked around and tried to right itself. By the next day at this time it would be in the stew pot, and it appeared to know that, carefully checking every avenue of escape. Rubia took the bird off the table and set it on the ground in the corner like any other commodity.

"Well, this will have to be our night bird, our messenger. This is not much for them to eat, but they just want the seed, the heart, that's all. We get the meat, not those 'things' in the cave. Now you have everything," she said, making a verbal inventory of the items that I had to take with me to the cave.

She had Lupe get out a *petate*, a large mat, to take along, and she carefully wrapped up all the things. She then explained again exactly how everything was to be done, how the offerings were to be placed, in what order the prayers were to be said, when the candles were to be lit, and how the actual sacrifice was to be made. She particularly emphasized what to do and not to do after I finished.

IT WAS ALREADY dark by the time I started out on the trail heading for the cave. Lupe had reluctantly agreed to go with me to show the way. It had been a long time since either of us had gone to this particular entryway to the underworld, which is not often visited by Sanmartinos. Once a year each family took offerings to the cave, leaving them on the ground in front but rarely venturing into even the mouth of the cave. Praying in the mouth of the cave, they believed, was assuredly a dangerous activity to be avoided if at all possible. Some would never leave their houses, simply leaving the offerings under their family altars, because the cold, evil winds of the north, emanating from the entries of the caves, could easily cause sickness and death.

Lupe was quite concerned about leaving her mother-in-law alone and intended to walk back to the village once I had made my way to the cave. As the jeep lurched and jolted over the trail in the night, I found I could not think about how foolish or absurd I might seem. The disease was real: I could show Rubia the diagnostic tests, and she would probably even understand them. But for her, it was her soul that was afflicted and lost, and she would not get better unless this matter was attended to. These cloudy connections between the "real" and the "unreal" confused and amazed me. For the second time in the Sierra, but for different reasons, I was finding it hard to use "metaphor" in my usual anthropological way.

We finally reached the path to the cave; in the darkness and overgrown by the forest, it was almost impassible.

"This is where we start out," Lupe said. She helped me carry everything from the truck down the twisting, narrow path to the cave. "Careful," she warned me, "'they' are everywhere here." She meant the supernaturals who inhabited the underworld. We both smoked constantly to ward off any of "them" who might be lurking in the undergrowth. We could feel the cool wind emanating from the dark, gaping mouth that was the entryway to the underworld. Our flashlights cast shadows like huge, moving teeth from the surrounding undergrowth. On one side of the grotto was an enormous rock that had obviously fallen long ago from the ceiling of the cave. This was the earth altar.

We had carried half the supplies down to the cave when Lupe decided to return home, her duty done. "Our grandmother is awaiting me," she explained. She really didn't want to go anywhere near the cave. She considered Rubia's tradition quite dangerous and had never shown any interest in embracing it. "Now is the time that I must leave you with 'them.' Be careful!"

Finally I got everything carried down and lit the torch, turning off the flashlight. Weird shadows leaped up in the dancing light, sometimes making everything seem huge and other times obscuring all but the gross details of the cave. I opened the *petate* and spread it out on the ground. Wax from old candles and black smudges of burned copal had been left from thousands of offerings and prayers before me. I noticed black obsidian flakes and plenty of *tepalcates*, pre-Columbian potsherds, on the ground and charred bones as well. All these were offerings for the Most Holy Earth. I tethered the young bird to a stake near the rock until I would need it. It kept a close watch on everything I did.

The sound of all my movements reverberated through the cave. My opening prayers of greeting echoed back and forth like an ancient choir. All of the voices searched with me for the reason that I was there. The ancestors had done this for generations. I thought about the religion of my own forebears; they would be aghast that I was here in this pagan place.

I began to make the offerings in the order that Rubia had prescribed. Each item was offered to the earth in the proper manner: thrown, as far as I could, deep into the blackness and down the cave's gullet into the bowels of the earth, which consumed the offerings. I could hear faint echoes, and once there was a splash of water.

The fatwood that Rubia had given me remained a blazing torch through the ordeal, though the cool, blowing winds snuffed out the candles almost as soon as they were lit. This was a good sign, however: the Lords of the underworld had heard my words.

The young black cock eyed me curiously as I started to go through the prayers in both Spanish and Nahuat. Every once in a while, it let out a loud crowing that resounded through the grotto. Its feathers shimmered in the faint light. It had long ago been given its "paper flag and feather headdress," the Aztec metaphor for one destined for sacrifice. I postponed taking care of the bird to the very end, but it had to be done. Rubia had told me just what I had to do, but that didn't make it any easier. I knew that we would eventually eat it, so Rubia's ritual propitiation of the earth was, in fact, preparation for dinner. Perhaps there was more to the absurd theory of protein capture as the basis for human sacrifice than I was willing to credit. But then again, perhaps sacrificial victims were simply tasty, or, as one anthropologist has suggested, death and ritual violence were the spice of life in the traditional world.

Rubia's instructions were quite specific. I grabbed the struggling, flapping bird and tried to split open its breast from the neck down with my pocketknife. It tried to wriggle free, but the blood and the contents of its crop shot out, and then Rubia's instructions became impossible to follow. I couldn't get to the heart through the bird's breast! Twisting and cutting, I used the knife to disembowel it, digging the guts out with my hand until at last I could reach up and grasp the heart. It had stopped beating. Everything inside was hot and slippery to the touch. I ripped open the body, pulled the heart off the vessels that held it, and tossed it into the cave, all the while proclaiming to the earth Lords that it was my own.

Then I had to pluck the bird. It is always easier to remove the feathers from a freshly killed bird, and Rubia, being a practical cook, wanted it plucked before being brought home. I had forgotten the Nahuat prayers, however, so, while feathers and blood were flying all over, I plucked away, furiously muttering Ave Marias and Pater Nosters from my Catholic childhood. What a mess this was! The black feathers stuck to the warm entrails on the ground in front of me, the smell of sputtering incense filled the air, the torch blazed away, and the blood on my hands and arms had started to get sticky as it dried.

Finally the ordeal was over, and I couldn't wait to leave. Most of the offerings had been made, but it was still several hours until dawn and I didn't want to climb the rough path to the jeep in the dark. I was hoarse from constant praying and smoking, so, putting out the torch to save it for the morning, I lay down on the damp and cold *petate*.

Fitful sleep consumed me as dreams wove themselves among semiconscious hallucinations.

Chapter 3

THE CURER

WHEN I AWOKE,
I HASTILY GATHERED EVERYTHING
TOGETHER, ROLLED
IT INTO THE PETATE, AND GROPED
MY WAY OUT OF THE CAVE.
It was a bright, sunny early morning,
and the trees were alive with
green parrots busily chatting.

I staggered up the trail, falling once and skinning my knee, climbed into the jeep, and somehow managed to drive back into town. Ignoring the stares of passersby, I got out at the plaza and walked up the hill. I was dirty, my clothing filthy with dried sweat and blood, and I was exhausted.

Don Inocente sat with Rubia on her stoop in the sunlight. Rubia seemed to be in much better spirits this morning. Her face was animated, and her eyes were lively as she spoke with Inocente. As soon as I got within earshot of the stoop, she asked me, "Have you ever seen something there in Talocan, in your dreams, that is big and dark?"

It was not exactly the right moment to try to recall my dreams. I was in the middle of the street, and I wasn't supposed to have slept last night. (I hardly did anyway.) Why didn't she ask me about the sacrifice, about how it went? I handed her the mangled corpse of the chicken, and she examined it briefly, as if in disgust, and handed it back to Lupe, who had come out of the kitchen to take a look.

"At least you plucked it," she said. "I think Lupe will make something tasty out of our messenger." Lupe stared down at the torn-up bird in dismay.

Some curious children also came over to gape. I felt more like Don Quixote than Saint Timothy, conquering hero, coming back from doing battle with the underworld.

"Well," I answered, "of course there are many things in dreams."

"No, but did something big and dark ever go after you, chase you down in dreams?"

"Well, 'they' are always chasing after *tonals* there," Inocente interjected, "maybe they have been chasing him for a long time."

"No, what I want to know is, if there is a witch, a *nagualli,* in there who's after me," Rubia replied.

"Of course there is a witch there. I told you there was a witch after you. That is surely what has got you," said Inocente.

"There is something that has my soul, my breath, my *tonal*," she said, coughing and wheezing. "And I want to know if he has ever seen 'those things' there, because if he can't see those things he won't do me any good," Rubia insisted. "Now did you ever dream of some big animal chasing you?" she asked.

"Not recently," I said, recalling a childhood nightmare when we lived on a farm in Wisconsin, "but there was a time long ago when I used to see a bull chasing me."

"There, you see," she said to Inocente, "I thought he could see those *nagualli* there, and he has seen them. He just doesn't recall what he was seeing."

"Maybe that was just a fright, a *susto,* when he was a child," Inocente said. "Did anyone go after your soul? Were you sick then?" he asked me.

"No, not that I can recall," I told the old man. Lupe came out with a chair for me to sit in. I was grateful.

"Didn't your parents ever take you to a healer after that?"

"Our healers are more like Arturo," I explained as I sat down, hoping that Lupe would bring us some coffee. "You go to them when you are sick, and they give you pills or stick you with a needle. They don't make offerings, or pray, or tell their dreams as you do."

I had seen enough curings and heard enough dream tales to know by then what Inocente was asking about. He was interpreting my childhood nightmares as a case of magical fright and soul loss, a common disease in the village that I had seen both Rubia and Inocente cure. As Rubia had become more receptive to my interest in her craft, she had insisted that I accompany her to the houses of children who were sick. She would spend the afternoon talking and gossiping while she arranged the family altar with offerings. Then she would pray to the saints and the Holy Earth, and afterward return home to try to find the child's lost soul in a dream. Inocente and Rubia wanted to know if I could recognize the earmarks of witchcraft in my dreams.

"See, that's what I thought. They have been chasing him for a long time now," Rubia said, "and no one ever went after his soul."

"But if he is still here with us, he must have found his soul, or else they couldn't really scare it out of him," Inocente said.

"If they didn't scare that soul out when he was a little one, then he has got a pretty tight hold on it." Rubia turned to me and asked, "Did you see that bull often? Do you ever see it now?"

Lupe finally came out with the thick, sweet coffee of the Sierra in steaming bowls. I had a moment to think as I blew on the coffee.

"I don't remember much about it now. All I really remember was that it was big and black and scary. It gave me a lot of nightmares."

"The bull was black, you say. All black?" she asked.

"I think so," I told her, "but that was many years ago. I don't really remember." The coffee was starting to perform its own magic.

"See, it really was a witch," Rubia said, turning to Inocente. "It couldn't scare the soul out of him, so it left him alone. His soul and his heart are well tied together; the ropes bind him well."

"That could be, but maybe it was just his own *nagual,* his animal, he was seeing," Inocente said.

"Doubt it," replied Rubia, "but it could be. I've never seen his animal soul there in Talocan."

"Neither have I. Think he knows it, what his *nagual* is?" Inocente asked Rubia.

"Doubt it," she said, "and we don't want to scare him off. I almost did that one time when he didn't come back to town for months."

Rubia was talking about 1974, when she had first begun to tell me about her dream traveling and prayers to the underworld. Afterward, I had left Mexico for nearly a year to begin graduate studies. She thought her discussions of the underworld had scared me from ever coming back to the village, but the following summer when I returned with considerable renewed interest, she was delighted. This was when she had begun teaching me some of the prayers and telling me her dreams.

"What else do you see in dreams?" Rubia asked rather cagily. She had never before asked me about my dreams.

"I don't know," I replied. The day was getting warmer. "I don't think much about them—unless they are quite exceptional. They are certainly not as interesting as your dreams."

"Nonsense," said Rubia, "your dreams are just like everyone else's. You just have to learn what you are really seeing. Talocan is a land of dusk and of dawn where nothing is ever really clear. There is a constant fog so that you don't really know what is before you. It's true that you don't know anyone there in the world of night, but all of those who have come before you are there. It is the world of our ancestors and yours too. If you follow the 'good path,' then you will find many allies there in the world of night."

"A lot of witches too!" interjected Inocente.

"Well, there are a lot of those things there, the *nagualli,* but following the 'good path' you will find many friends and brothers who will protect you. First you must learn the places in Talocan that you can go to. You must follow the ways the ancestors have shown us to live a good life. If you pray, as we do, with gifts for them, you will not be harmed in the world of dreams. You will be protected both by the Lords of the darkness and by our ancestors. You offered them your heart last night. Now you must discover if they will let you see in their world of darkness. Lupe!" she called out. "Bring him more coffee.

"You will have to ask the saints in the church for their help this morning. Their holy light will help protect you. You will have to go down to the church and ask San Miguel and San Juan, light of the morning and the evening, for their help! San Martín and Santiago, too, will be able to help. Each of them will need candles, flowers, and a bit of cash. Then there are your ancestors. Do you have any pictures of them?

"No, I don't," I replied.

"I'll show you how to pray to them right here. It's easy. You need to get some things that 'they' want down there, but Lupe can help with that. You won't need another bird. This one looks good enough for today. We'll give 'em a bite of it in *chilpotzontli* sauce," she said slyly. This was how she and Lupe were going to cook last night's chicken. Chicken was a real treat in the village, for there were few of them. Villagers rarely ate meat; it was far too expensive.

"Well," Inocente remarked, "he's going to have to know what part of him goes in the darkness."

"He already does," Rubia said, turning to me and asking, "where is the part that goes into the night?"

"Wellll," I said, blowing out a long breath, "it is right here inside all of us." I used strictly correct Nahuat terms. "It's that spark of the life that moves about in the night."

"Well, he knows!" Inocente said. "You've taught him a lot already. I never told him that."

"Sure you did, Inocente," I replied. "You always said it was the *tonal* that went into the night."

"No, it must have been this old witch who told you about that," he joked.

Rubia came right back at him. "Who's the old witch around here, you old fart!" Turning back to me, she demanded, "Tell this old witch about souls, and which ones travel in the night." At this point Lupe emerged with more coffee. The Aztec concept of a soul is a difficult matter, and this was the second time that morning I was grateful for Lupe's timing.

I lit a cigarette, blew on the coffee, and leaned back on the rickety chair. "This is what I know about souls," I began, "from what you have told me and what I understand. People have three souls. First there is the heart, the *yollo*, and that is the life of the body. It is the movement within the body, that which gives us life and movement. Without the heart, the body does not stir; it does not move; one is dead.

"Then there is the *tonal*. That is the spark of life, the heat that animates the body. The *tonal* is the first light of dawn when we are born, the spark of light that is the first face of the sun that we see. It is our luck, our fate. But the *tonal* is not always held well by the body. It can be scared out of the body by a fall or a sudden knock on the head, and at night in dreams it can travel to places like the underworld. It can be captured by witches, or by those creatures that live 'down there,' the *ajmotocnihuan*, 'those who are not our brothers.'"

I drew deeply on my cigarette and poured the hot coffee into myself. I was straining to use the proper terms in Nahuat. I turned to Lupe and gave her my empty bowl to refill.

"Down there, in the underworld," I said, "there is also an animal that is born when we are born, on the same day, at the same moment. Each of us has one. Some are tigers, some are dogs, some are other things. We share the same fate with them. We are born under the same face of the sun. We share the same *tonal*. These are the *naguals* that are kept by the Lord of the animals in great corrals in Talocan. The Lord of the animals cares for them and protects his animals. He keeps them safe there, and he will help those who will help him protect his animals. In this way he protects us too, just as the Lords of the Most Holy Earth nourish and sustain us here on the earth. What happens to someone's *nagual* also happens to his or her heart and body."

Lupe came out with more coffee. I set my bowl on the stones of the stoop and looked into Rubia's piercing black eyes.

"Why do they keep the *naguals* there?" Inocente asked me.

These two frail old people, one nearly blind, the other on death's doorstep, were relentless inquisitors. I was feeling a little the way I used to when I had to recite my catechism correctly for the priests and nuns of my childhood.

"Because every once in a while," I answered, "a *nagual* will escape, and this can be very dangerous. If the *nagual* is hurt or injured, or if a witch should do it some harm, the person suffers the exact same damage. We each have different hearts, but we share the *tonal* with our *nagual*. I don't know much about the *nagual*, the animal, but it seems to me to be a part of the soul. I think that it shares the *tonal* with a person. No?" I was still very unsure of myself. Now I felt more as though I were reciting my Credo in Latin as an acolyte: unreal and abstract. It was hard to think about this unless I thought of the underworld as real. Inocente and Rubia both knew it was real, but it was hard for me to go along. I recalled how the faith of my childhood had slipped away long ago.

"Sounds like he may be able to see there in Talocan," Inocente commented.

"Well, he seems to know that it is what is in his heart, his *yollo*, that gives him his life here on the earth," Rubia said more to me than to Inocente. "The *yollo* is the heart that is returned to the earth when life is finished. The heart is the seed, the core of life. From it, life sprouts forth. In the heat and light of the sun, the *tonal* sprouts and grows. The *tonal* gives us our life when we are born, our luck and our fate. The *tonal* is the part of us that goes everywhere. It lives in Talocan; it lives on the earth, in Talticpac. It lives in the sky in Ilhuicac, but it is only well on earth or in the sky with the sun. The *tonal* is that spark of life that is us. It is what makes you you and me me. The *nagual* is the other self. It is the other me, or the other you, and you share your life, and your *tonal,* with it. It is the *nagual* that you must know, and the *tonal* is what you need to find, because it is your *tonal* that moves about in dreams. You must know what the heart, the *tonal,* sees to find the *nagual,* the animal," she told me. "You must have had more than that one dream about a black bull."

Did she think this was my *nagual?* "I . . . I don't remember, Rubia. When I was a child I saw it more than once, but I have not seen it for many years."

"Sounds like 'they' are keeping his dreams there in the darkness in their worlds of night," she said to Inocente. "It looks as if he's going to have to do something special to bring those dreams back on his shoulders, to carry that burden into the light. He'll have to find a way to get them to let him take them out. The *alpixque* can do that, but he will have to leave offerings for them at the water." She pulled a stray wisp of her white hair back and tucked it in among her wound braids.

"The *tepehuane,* the 'hill people,' could be a help, too," Inocente said. "Those 'things' are all over here."

"Well, he went to the cave last night, and they should be happy with what he gave them there. They did get the seed, the heart, of our tasty little night bird," Rubia said. "I can't understand, though, how he's never seen anything in the world of darkness. He dreams like everyone else. He just doesn't remember them."

"Maybe he's not even back from the cave yet," Inocente commented. "Maybe they actually got him and kept his *tonal* down there. He could be here sitting with us, and they could still have his *tonal* in the darkness."

"What did you do in there?" Rubia asked me.

"I said the prayers and put out the offerings the way you showed me."

"It took you all night just to say the prayers?" she asked rather incredulously.

"Well, it took a while to pluck the bird for you," I told her.

"Pluck it! You tore the thing apart and nearly skinned it. That couldn't have taken you so long at all."

"Did he have plenty of tobacco in there with him?" Inocente asked.

"Sure did," Rubia said.

"Yes, but was there enough smoke to keep those others away from him all night?"

"Sure was, if he didn't stop smoking. You kept on puffing away all night; there was enough smoke there, right?"

"Yes, yes," I replied, "except toward morning, after I plucked the bird I felt a bit sleepy."

"You didn't go to sleep in there! I warned you that they are eaters of our flesh there. You didn't sleep there!"

"Toward morning I may have dozed off for a few minutes," I said.

"That's it!" Inocente said. "They got him, and they're keeping him there. Now we'll have to find another lost soul in the darkness. This one didn't really come out at all." He paused. "Well, maybe they didn't get him, but I am sure they got a good look at him, and they will surely be wanting a taste of more than that night bird of ours. He can't go back down to the cave—not now at least, when those things are waiting for him there. They would surely get him then. It looks as though he's going to have to find out if his soul was taken last night. He's going to have to go back to that cave in his dreams, but he's going to have to sleep here where it's safe, in front of the altar. If he's still got his *tonal,* he is going to have to go back to Talocan. He's got to dream tonight. He's also got to go with something more than prayers. They already got the chicken, so they are well fed there in the cave. Maybe we can get them drunk down there."

"He took some *aguardiente* last night, but tonight he'll need a whole liter!" Rubia said. "You are going to have to return to the cave in your dreams tonight and find your own way out of that place.

"You won't last long on this earth if they do have your *tonal* down there. If you dozed off, they at least got a good look at you. You are going to have to take on the burden of service to them. You'll have to offer them things that they need in the darkness, or else they will keep you, and then your path is finished, your light will be extinguished here on this earth." She was beginning to wheeze. Her early morning enthusiasm had exhausted her.

"If you think after this you can get away from 'them,' you are wrong," she continued nevertheless. "They'll find your soul. You are going to have to learn how to get around in their world of night now. I think about a liter of *aguardiente* should be enough for tonight, but you're going to need some powerful help getting in and out of Talocan. You're going to have to visit the saints, and you're going to need their help," she told me and coughed again. "Lupe can get us the offerings, and you'll have to go over to see Don Pedro for that liter of *aguardiente.*"

"All right, but, Doña Rubia, I want you to rest," I insisted.

The urgency with which Doña Rubia was instructing me made me rather nervous. Never before had she been so insistent about what had to be done. She wanted to come with me to the village church, but both Lupe and I insisted that she stay and conserve her strength. Inocente didn't seem to care one way or another about it, and I wondered why.

I WENT DOWN to the village church of San Martín by myself, as Rubia had instructed. There I prayed most of the morning. I

prayed in Spanish, Latin, and Nahuat. I said the Credos, Ave
Marias, and Pater Nosters I remembered from my days as an altar
boy. Rubia was fond of the old way of praying in Latin. There was
somehow a great affinity between this and her prayers in Nahuat
that I was also beginning to feel. After finishing the prayers, I left
offerings for almost every saint in the church.

When I returned, Inocente had left, and Lupe had finished
cooking the bird. She had also got all the necessary offerings, which
were neatly stacked on Doña Rubia's altar.

Rubia rose from her pallet in the kitchen for lunch, which we
ate at the table in front of the altar while Lupe served us. All
through the meal, Doña Rubia insisted on telling me precisely how
the Lords of the underworld had to be addressed. They had to be
implored and bribed in order to make sure that they would not keep
my soul or send out their minions in search of it. She was obviously
very concerned; there was no question of my not becoming a
servant of the Lords of the earth. It was simply what had to be done.

It was already late afternoon when Inocente returned with his
son, Lucas.

"You have everything there?" the old seer asked, for he couldn't
see well enough to notice what was on the altar.

"I still have to get the *aguardiente*," I replied, "but everything
else is there. The tobacco, the flowers, the incense, a dish of
chilpotzontli—some tortillas and beans, too."

Rubia had also rearranged the pictures of the saints on her altar
so that Saint Michael and Saint John were more prominent, but
Inocente couldn't see that.

She came out of the kitchen and said to him, "Are you going to
get to work and start praying, or are you just going to sit there?" To
me, she ordered, "Now, go up to Pedro's and get that bottle of
alcohol. We're going to start the praying before the holy light is

gone, so that you can begin to work there in the darkness." What she meant was that I could begin to dream. I was glad to hear that this was not going to be another sleepless night.

By the time I got back with the bottle, which was now only partly full—Don Pedro and I had each had several *copitas* at his store before he would let me return—Rubia and Inocente were well into a long litany to the Lords of the earth and the sky. I joined them in the dark altar room, and the three of us prayed for several hours. Alternating with the prayers, we made offerings by throwing broken cigarettes and small shot glasses of liquor into the smoldering censer on her altar, which made wretched smells and loud hisses. Then we would pass one another the bottle and fill our own small glasses. Occasionally we would add more guttering candles to the many that were already there on the altar, their hot wax running in rivulets across the fresh oilcloth that Lupe had placed on the table in preparation for the night. Then, we would pray, drink, and smoke some more. As we watched through the open door into the kitchen, the white stucco turned from yellow to orange in the dimming light of the setting sun.

Evening came, and the embers of the hearth created a faint glow in the kitchen. When it had become too dark to see, instead of turning on the single bulb hanging from the ceiling, Lupe lit five candles around the kitchen. In their half-light, she prepared and brought us some food, small pieces of which were also offered to the fire. By the time we finished eating, it was well past ten, and we were all fairly drunk.

We congratulated one another effusively on our performance, but I had the feeling that our camaraderie was masking some uneasiness, as well. I was too drunk to think about this. Inocente's loyal son helped him out the door, and the two of them unsteadily descended the old path to their house.

Rubia motioned me to the bench in the main room where the altar was that I used on nights I couldn't return to Quetzalan. I preferred it to the straw mats, which were always filled with biting insects that Rubia never seemed to notice.

"With all those prayers, those *alpixque,* 'the water ones,' will surely help you," she reassured me.

My head was spinning.

Rubia's final words to me that night were, "Just make sure they do not keep you there."

Chapter 4

TALOCAN

THE ACRID, PINEY SMOKE
OF COPAL INCENSE
HUNG IN THE AIR
mixed with the stale smell of tobacco smoke.
All night a single votive candle burned
on the altar table,
casting eerie, moving shadows
on the portraits of saints and ancestors.

Many times that night I awoke in the candle's strange, yellowish glow. The flickering of the light on the saints and ancestors contrasted with the absolute darkness under the altar, where the earth Lords dwelt. These visions and the events of the day entered into and influenced my dreams, I am certain, but there were other things in them that I couldn't really see or remember clearly.

There was the cave where I had been the night before, the great, gaping mouth of the earth that I had entered, the cathedral of the Most Holy Earth that reverberated with choruses of my prayers and incantations. The hissing, sputtering sound of the copal filled me with smoky images of ancient arches, chapels, and shrines. One of the times I awakened, I remembered serving mass when I was young. A fellow acolyte had collapsed from the smoke and rigors of the litany of an interminable high mass and benediction. When I returned to my dreams, a huge and horrible figure resplendent in gold-and-red priestly robes stood before me. Putting his hand on my shoulder, he threw me into a whirlwind of unknown faces.

There were great halls and houses around me as I walked away from the facade of a church much like the cathedral of San Francisco in Quetzalan. I remembered walking through fog and mist down darkened cobblestone streets that I had traversed many times before, but there was not a soul in sight, and there was no light.

A man in white native dress came out of the dark. His face was not distorted the way all the others in my dreams had been. The face was not clear, but his eyes danced like Inocente's. He had a short black mustache like my grandfather's and shimmering black hair. He was obviously a Sanmartino by the way he dressed, but I didn't recognize him as anyone I knew.

He was calling out to me in Nahuat, and at first I couldn't hear him, though he was clearly shouting. Finally I was able to understand him.

"Xihuiqui nican! Come here!" he cried.

"Where?"

"Here! Here! Here!" He was motioning with his head and his lips the way Sanmartinos do.

I was confused and hesitated, perhaps half-seeing the shadows dancing off the huge white flowers onto the walls behind Rubia's altar. Then I was whirling after the little man, but not moving. There were clusters of white flowers everywhere as we seemed to flow along through the misty dream world. There were no more distorted faces or dark crags, halls, towers, or cathedrals. Now there were flowers and the lush vegetation that surrounded the hills of Quetzalan everywhere—the camellias of Dr. Moran's garden and the orchids of his neighbor, Mrs. Salazar.

We settled on a grassy knoll, and for the first time things were becoming clearer. I could see the lights of a dozen little villages on surrounding hilltops in the night. Everything was shimmering.

The enigmatic little figure told me to sit down, and I did.

"I live here," he said. "I have my house here. It's just over there!"

I stretched out. I was lying flat on the hard ground. It was rough, and I was uncomfortable.

"Come over here!" he said, but I was feeling very nervous, perhaps because of Rubia's and Inocente's stories about the *ajmotocnihuan,* "those who are not our brothers," who trick people into the cave.

"What is your name?" I called out to him, but he had begun to recede into the darkness. I thought I heard him shout out, "Cruz!" Then I was on a high Golgotha, a hill covered with bones. Everywhere I stepped, I heard the crunching of bones and skulls underfoot. It was dark, and there were sparks and then wails as I began to run down the hill. I fell into a whirling spiral with the skulls and bones all around me. The noise was such that I was tossing and turning, and I could not awaken. I saw the great hairy priest in his golden cloak again and all the faces that I had seen earlier in the night. The two acolytes were bearing another splendorous vestment for the dark priest. I ran from the cathedral back to the now deserted village. As I stumbled over the cobblestones, I saw the great houses and halls turn to native huts. I was on the path through the great ferns that I took every morning from Quetzalan to San Martín. It was still dark, and I was beginning to awaken.

I could hear Lupe in the kitchen addressing the three fire dogs of the hearth, the three stones that she rested her pots and griddle on, so that she could safely light the morning fire. There was more rustling, and the daily miracle of coffee appeared. I profusely thanked the kind woman. She retreated back into the kitchen, and I was left alone with my thoughts. I sat drinking, hunched over on the hard bench. As the light began to show through the cracks of the still-barred door in the windowless room, I wondered how I was going to relate to Rubia what had happened. I thought about this for a while. Finally I decided on a series of episodes, rather than a continual stream of events, as the best way to look at the dream. I knew how dream tales were told, and in my still sleepy mood I began to forge this one into an acceptable narrative that my mentor would understand.

I heard Rubia call me, and I struggled to my feet to make my way to the back of the house. She was propped up on her pallet, and Lupe was braiding her hair. The room still smelled of sickness, but she seemed much better.

"So . . . you dreamed! Well . . . get on with it!" she said. "Sit down and tell me!" She motioned me to a low stool. I sat down, rubbing my eyes.

"Well . . . " I began, "there was the cave." I paused and began again, "I entered into the dream in a cave. I think it was the same cave that I was in the night before. There was a huge, gaping mouth with vines and stones covering the floor."

"Yeesss," Rubia commented, drawing the word out—this was a standard way to ask the narrator for more information in Sierra Nahuat tale telling. I began to expand on my story in the correct style of Nahuat for telling these things.

"The vines were teeth hanging from the top of the grotto. The inside was black and dark. In the cave was the darkest night, with no stars or moon. The stones were huge and black, covered with soot and smoke. It was a place of night, not the night of this earth but of eternal night."

"Yes, that is the darkness of Talocan," said Rubia. "Sooo . . . you see, you *can* find your way into the Most Holy Earth. That is how to enter their world of night. I think you can do this. You can get into their world of darkness. Now you have to learn to see what is there and how to get around in the darkness." She was obviously quite pleased. "Now, come on. Tell me what else you saw in there."

"Well, it was like a great dark cathedral there on the inside, and they were praying. There was smoke everywhere. I could see the baptistery and the shrines there, all black and covered with soot. There was plenty of smoke in there, enough to make you fall over. I was kneeling at the altar, and there was a great, large priest with a huge gold cloak, chanting. The priest was in front of me, so that I could only see his back. There were others there in white and in black, all praying, but I couldn't understand them. The altar was high and shiny, not gold but maybe silver. It sparkled, and I could not see much of it in the smoke. One of the acolytes fell over. Everyone there was praying except me, and then the priest turned. He was big and black with large eyes, and he threw me into the faces that were praying there. Things were swirling, and then I was outside the cathedral on a street."

"What were they doing in the cathedral?" she asked urgently. "Was it a wake? A wake with candles, a *velada?* That's how they catch souls down there, and that's how they keep them. They hold a vigil for the soul until the person dies, and then they eat the flesh. That is their nourishment there in the world of darkness. We eat from the earth, and then the earth eats us. That's what they do there."

"No it wasn't a funeral, or a vigil," I said. "It was more like a high mass or a benediction with plenty of smoke and incense."

"When you got out of there, were you in a village, or a city?" she asked.

"Well, at first there were great halls and houses of cities, but as I went along it was just a cobblestone street. There was no light."

"How did you get there?" she asked. "Did you walk, or were you blown by the winds? Were you floating in the waters?"

This was something that I had never thought about, how one moved about in dreams. It seemed very important to Rubia, so I told her that I must have been blown by the winds, as I didn't remember walking on the cobblestone streets.

"You see, they took you there. The winds took you out from the chapel and showed you their town. There are fourteen towns, fourteen villages, fourteen cities, there in the world of darkness. At the heart of Talocan, in the center of that flower of the night, there is one village, one town, one county seat, one city, and one capital. That is where you have to go to find the True Taloc, the Lord of the worlds of darkness. It is Ipalnemoani, 'him by whom we live,'" she said, using the same name the Aztecs had used in the sixteenth century.

Lupe had finished with Rubia's hair and adjusted her bedding. She was sitting up straight now and kept on talking.

"He grants us life here on the earth, and justice. He is our food and our sustenance. To find him you have to find the four sides of Talocan and then the heart of the world of darkness." Her cadence, as she told me this, was almost like recitation of a prayer, yet she said it with such urgency that I knew these were her deepest beliefs. "Now where did you go there in the town? It wasn't a village and it wasn't a city, but a cathedral like that is where they say the high masses. It must have been some kind of county seat. So, you found an important place where they live there in the earth, and they didn't want to take you or eat you. You may learn to dream well."

At this point I was quite pleased with myself and continued on. "As I went along the street, the great houses and halls dwindled and became more like the houses here in San Martín, with thatched roofs and stone walls around. Then there was a man with a little mustache on the road, and he was calling out to me. I think his name was Cruz, or something like that."

"What?" she interjected. "He told you his name! He was not one of 'them.' This is something we have to talk to Inocente about. Never say that you have seen such people there. Inocente can tell you why. You must be very careful about this. What did this man tell you?"

"He said to come with him," I replied, no longer telling the tale but trying to simply describe what had happened. "I followed the man, and we went along past some flowers. They were huge white flowers, and we ended up on a hill where I could see other villages in the night. The man told me his house was near and that I should come with him. I didn't want to. You have told me all those stories about how 'they' trick you into the cave to be consumed, and I didn't want to follow him."

"Well, if he had a name, he sure wasn't one of 'them.' If this man lives there in Talocan, he's probably not alive anymore, but Inocente will know more about that," she said slowly, getting up. "Must be someone's ancestor, but whose? There are a lot of Cruzes around. Why does he want you there?" the old woman muttered in a general way, more to herself than to me, as if she were thinking out loud.

She called to Lupe, who was now in the kitchen, "I'm going down to Inocente's with Timoteo."

On our way out of the house, Rubia took from the altar an old shoulder bag and some of the cigarettes, along with a candle. She also wrapped a small handful of incense in a section of banana leaf.

"Let's go!" she said. "You may have to help me over those stones on the way. I am weak, but Inocente has to hear about this. He can tell us what to do now."

It was a bright morning with just an occasional cloud hanging onto the hills around the village. As we walked out of Rubia's house, just a few doors up from the center of the town, people were staring at us. I must have been quite a sight: all I had to wear were the torn, bloodstained clothes I'd worn in the cave. Doña Rubia took slow, deliberate steps. I helped her along. With a slow determination she smiled at everyone and greeted them. It was with good reason that she was known in town as everyone's grandmother.

As we came around the side of the old school building and turned down the rutted path toward Inocente's house, she hesitated, picking her way among the stones. I helped her over some of the deeper ruts in the road, and we continued on. There were children playing out in front of their houses, and she seemed to know them all. She had probably helped to deliver most of them, being a popular, well-known midwife in the village. She smiled at the children and inquired about their parents as we went, but I was the major focus of their curiosity. They were probably asking one another what this disheveled-looking gringo was doing helping a frail old woman through the streets.

By the time we got down to Inocente's house, an entire posse of children was following us, laughing and joking and trying to test my

Nahuat with obscene or semiobscene little phrases. Rubia, too, was enjoying the passel of followers we had gathered, warning the children whenever they got a bit too boisterous that she would have to visit their mothers.

"*Tanesic*, the light has come," she called out to Lucas as we approached Inocente's house. Lucas was out on the front stoop with his eldest son, who was about nine years old. They were waiting for some men to arrive with firewood.

"Well, is the old man up?" Rubia asked.

"Sure is! He's right inside," Lucas said.

At that same moment we heard Inocente call out, "What are you doing here so early? Must have been quite a night, Timoteo." I had not spoken yet, but he knew that I was there. Inocente always had a way of knowing everything that was going on around him. "Come in, and recount the night."

As we went in, he got up from his seat and made his way over to his altar, on the way reaching for a chair for me. He always insisted that I use the one Western chair in his house. He pulled out another low native stool for Doña Rubia and called out to Elena, Lucas's wife, to bring coffee. I helped Rubia to sit down.

"It's fresh this morning. I toasted the beans myself," he told us. Elena brought out the coffee, and we savored it for a few minutes.

"Well, he did it, all right!" Rubia suddenly began. "He went right straight into the cave—the one I sent him to, the Eastern Mouth of Earth. The winds took him in, I think. He doesn't know too much about that yet, but it had to be the winds, or the *popocamej*. He said there was a lot of smoke in there. Could have been the *popocamej* who led him in there."

"You sure it was the Eastern Earth Mouth?" Inocente asked. "It could have been the Stone Mouth or the Water-Earth Mouth. There are plenty of doors to the world of darkness." Inocente went into a long discourse about all the entrances to the underworld.

Rubia told me to listen carefully about the entryways that I would have to use to get in and out of the underworld: some were for men, and some were for women; others were the provinces of particular supernaturals; others pertained to the winds, the waters, the smoke, or the earth. I was trying to remember all I was being told by going over and over it in my mind; I had no notepad.

"So, you think it was the Eastern Earth Mouth where he went in?" Inocente asked Rubia. "Where do *you* think it was, Don Timoteo?"

I replied that it seemed to be the same cave I had prayed in.

"You know, he went right into a benediction there in the Most Holy Earth. He was kneeling and praying right there on the altar, and the dark priest threw him out," Rubia went on.

"Well, he's lucky they didn't keep him there for lunch, to feed on. They were probably praying for someone else to be sent, maybe even you," Inocente commented to Rubia.

Rubia ignored the remark and continued, "He was blown out of the cathedral onto a street with great houses, along a path. Then he began to see houses like ours. That's where he was confronted by this 'thing.'" Rubia used the impersonal particle in Nahuat.

"Was it one of them, or was it one of us?" Inocente asked.

"I think it was one of us," the old woman declared.

"One of us? Hmmmm," said Inocente.

"He said there was a name he heard that 'thing' shout. It was 'Cruz.'"

I looked at Rubia, wondering why she had mentioned the name, when she had just told me that I shouldn't ever mention it.

"Well, better not tell anyone about that," Inocente declared. "There are Cruzes who live down there below the town well. They wouldn't like this at all. Does Timoteo know how dangerous this is?"

"I don't think so. You tell him. You know their ways better."

Turning to me, Inocente switched into Spanish, "So you saw a man named Cruz. You must never tell anyone that you have seen the living or the dead in your dreams," he said with great finality, glancing over at Rubia. "They are there all right, but even when you see them you can't tell anyone.

"If it's a living person that you see, and you are not working especially to cure him, it is probably a lost soul dreaming, too. You could take it, if you were a witch," he said with certainty. "You could offer that lost soul to 'them,' the Lords of night, and bind them in obligation to you. They would owe you something for that, another favor or, perhaps, another soul.

"If it's not a lost soul," Inocente went on, "then it means that this soul is probably a witch trying to harm someone. If 'they' hear about that, then they'll get you. If it is the dead that you see, then you may be out to do harm to someone's ancestors, and he or she will hire a witch to get you.

"You can never mention the souls of this earth that you see in the underworld. Either you will be called a witch, or you will be witched, if you talk about them.

"You can tell us," he said emphatically, "about those souls you see in the world of night, but tell no one else." Inocente then wanted more information about "Cruz."

Rubia was becoming a little edgy about this insistence. "That's his business, not yours, you old witch," Rubia finally said.

"Just shut up!" the old man snapped in Nahuat. "If it is one of the Cruz ancestors, I want to know which one. If it was one of those witches, there may be trouble, and we don't want to scare this young man off. He doesn't know their ways yet."

"I want to know how Timoteo got out of there into the light again. Forget about Cruz. We'll find out more later. Or are you afraid of them still?" Rubia commented slowly. "They haven't done any damage for a loooong tiiiime." I thought back to two years ago, when I had taped Inocente contracting to do witchcraft.

"He has to know all the ways in and out of Talocan before he can find the four sides of the underworld. He has to be able to get in and out if he is going to follow the path in his dreams. If he learns the 'good path,' he won't need to worry about Cruz," she said to Inocente. "After Cruz left, what did you see there?" Rubia asked me.

I was a bit hesitant to tell them about the mountain of bones, but I decided that it was part of the dream and that it would be interesting to see what they made of it. I recounted the story of walking across the bones and then seeing the dark priest again and escaping to the path that leads to the village.

Rubia and Inocente were of the opinion that the "priest" was praying for more souls to be sent to the underworld, and Rubia was particularly interested in this. She openly wondered if they were looking and waiting for her soul. Inocente said that he thought they were. He thought that a witch had promised it to them in the world of darkness.

"If that is what they were doing, then they will probably be satisfied with some other offering. I just might be able to get my own soul back myself," she said coyly, not telling Inocente how she would do that. I thought that perhaps she would need another chicken. The old man was of the opinion that it was definitely witchcraft and she could do nothing about it.

Both Rubia and Inocente agreed, however, that this first dream had been a very eventful journey into Talocan, and they took it upon themselves to explain just what had really happened in the world of darkness.

Rubia began: "You entered Talocan through the Eastern Earth Mouth, and the winds took you directly to the cathedral in one of the fourteen county seats of the underworld. There you were cast out, for you were not what they wanted. You were helped by a man there, and then you followed him to the hill near his house in Talocan. He was one of the ancestors and would not have led you astray, but you did not know this. The winds then swept you to the bone mountain of Miquitalan, the land where the dead enter the Most Holy Earth. The priest was praying for a new soul to be placed in the earth."

"He cast him out, though, that dark priest did," Inocente said. "This is good. They do not want him there in the world of darkness, and they are not keeping his soul there. He came out on the good path. If he follows this, then he will be able to enter many times and find the ways of the underworld and the ancestors. First he has to learn the entries and exits, then the four sides. Then he must see the True Taloc, the center, if he is to be of service to them."

"But how do I find all these pathways to Talocan?" I asked Inocente.

"First you must learn to see clearly in your dreams through the darkness and fog."

"But how will I even know where I am?"

"The same way you know where you are here on the earth," Rubia explained. "There is everything in Talocan that there is here on the earth, only because you cannot see clearly there in the darkness, any one place can lead to any other place. They are all together between the center and the sides."

"What?" I was not at all understanding what she was trying to explain.

"There is everything there that is on the earth," she repeated.

"Yes," said Inocente chuckling, "there is even a Mexico City and a Paris there in the darkness, or at least that's what they tell me. I haven't been to those places."

"But how will I know these places?"

"We will tell you," the old man replied.

"But how will I know where to go in Talocan?" I asked, becoming totally confused.

"You will not know," Rubia replied. "It is a land of darkness. Talocan is a great flower of darkness." She began pointing with a stick on the dirt floor of Inocente's house, beginning to trace a large, squared flower.

"The North is the Cave of the Winds, Ejecatalan or Ejecatan, and the Land of the Dead, Miquitalan or Mictali," she said, drawing a petal. "The East is the Sea, Apan." She drew another petal. "The South is the Land of Heat, Atotonican." She glanced up, then drew another petal. "The West is the House of the Women, the Cihuauhchan in Tonallan," she said as she drew the final petal. "Here in the center is the true heart of Talocan, the Talocan Melaw." She completed her diagram. "This is the way the underworld is," she said.

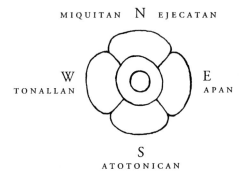

MIQUITAN   N   EJECATAN

W
TONALLAN

E
APAN

S
ATOTONICAN

What Rubia had drawn was the large square flower that has decorated the Mexican world since the time of Teotihuacan. I had seen the same design in ancient codices and on crumbling temple walls. I was astounded.

"Inside this are fourteen of everything, as I have told you," she said. "Thirteen outside the center for us, and one of everything inside for the Lords. But inside and outside are all the same, they are not separate there. Why, there is even a flower inside us, if we look for it there," she said enigmatically, but did not elaborate.

As the morning passed, Rubia and Inocente explained over and over the ways of entering and leaving the underworld through caves, streams, pools, sinkholes, and wells. The flower on the floor was so marked with lines by the end of the morning that it was almost totally obscured.

Scattered among the dream tales I had heard in curing ceremonies were many of these entries and exits, but now I saw how Rubia and Inocente used them to revise my dream tale to fit their vision of the underworld. These were the things I was expected to see in dreams. I was awed by these two old sages.

I told them that I could not stay in the Sierra for more than another day (I had classes to teach in Mexico City), but they said that if I had an altar and a place to pray, I could dream anywhere, even in Mexico City. What was important, they both explained to me, was that I remembered each dream, that I could "bear the dream into the light" so they could tell me where I had gone in the underworld. I eagerly agreed to keep a dream journal and arranged to stay in touch with Rubia by telephone.

We left Inocente's in the early afternoon. Elena was pleased, I am sure, that we did not stay for *comida*. There was never enough food in the house, and she would have had to go out and make great expenditures if we were to stay: Rubia was a *comadre* who had to be treated well, and I was an honored guest.

As we walked slowly back to Rubia's, the sly old sorceress commented, "You know, Inocente is wrong that there's a witch, unless he's the witch himself.

"If 'they' are still praying for souls to be sent to them there in Talocan," she said a little later, with a knowing glimmer in her clear, dark eyes, "then they haven't really made a deal with a witch, or at least not a good deal. I know what they want down there, what they need down there, and I can give them more. I can make a better deal. I know what they need there in the darkness," she stated flatly.

I left Lupe and Rubia before lunch. I explained to Lupe that Rubia had to take her medication and told her I would talk to Arturo when I got back to Quetzalan to see if he could find anything better for the old woman. Rubia was exhausted and went back to her pallet before I left.

As I drove back over the rough jeep trail to Quetzalan, I picked up as many people walking along the road as the old jeep I had borrowed from the university would hold. Among them was Don Ignacio, who lived on the way to the graveyard at the entrance to town. He was one of the town's great gossips. Everyone in the truck talked about the town and the festivals of the last year, taking little heed of my disheveled appearance. As my packed vehicle emptied out, Ignacio drew me aside, warning, "You've been out with those two old witches again. Better learn how to take care of yourself." He made his hand into a pistol. "Pam! They're killers all right, but they don't kill with a gun."

After I had left everyone at the main square, I went to pick up my bags at the hotel and then stopped at Arturo's before beginning the long drive back to Mexico City. Though the treacherous mountain roads required slow, cautious driving, I was distracted as I wound my way up to the highlands. My thoughts were filled with visions of the cave, the chorus of prayers, my fuzzy memories of dreams, and all that had happened in the last few days. Don Ignacio's warning and the two old seers' insistence that I embrace their tradition also weighed heavily on me.

I wondered what Rubia's altar would be like that night. I was sure she would be taking her case to the Lords of darkness, seeking justice and making lavish offerings for them as she tried to outbid her rival. Had my dream really given her the key to save her own lost soul? They wanted me to learn this for some reason. Both had worked with other anthropologists who were studying their ways in the Sierra, and up until now Rubia and Inocente, especially Rubia, had been free enough with their knowledge. Never, however, had any anthropologist I had known about been asked to dream. Was it only because I spoke Nahuat? Or was it because they expected me to find *my* lost soul down there?

Chapter 5

THE *NAGUAL*

THE RETURN TO MEXICO CITY AND
TEACHING WAS UNEVENTFUL.
MY OWN DREAMS COULD NOT COMPARE
with the tales that the two old curers had told me
of epic battles, near-death experiences,
and incredible escapes from pursuit by malevolent supernaturals
from Talocan,
the world of dreams.

I kept up my dream journal, trying each morning to string together the jumbled events of the night before. There were friends, relatives, familiar and unfamiliar places, but nothing really unusual—no massive pyramids or bloody sacrifices. The ancient Aztecs whose tradition I was to follow, with their lost books of dreams, did not take over my nights.

I waited a week, and still there was nothing, so I called Rubia at the appointed time. She wasn't there. Finally, I called Arturo, and he sent a message to her by another villager. Arturo also mentioned that Rubia appeared much better, responding to the new medication, which I hoped she was taking regularly.

Making a long-distance phone call from Mexico City at that time was no small task. It was necessary to go to either the offices of the National Telephone Company or another authorized long-distance station and wait endlessly for an operator, who never seemed to answer, then wait even longer to get the long-distance station in Quetzalan, where the operator answered only sporadically. I would leave a message to be delivered—or not—depending on the whims of the operator and the messenger and then begin the whole process over again. I usually sat in Sanborn's on the Reforma, near the *Monument to Independence* (better known as the *Angel*), sipping coffee and watching the tourists as I waited endless hours for calls to go through.

When I finally did get Rubia on the telephone, it was about a week later. She was not at all shy or overwhelmed by the mechanics of phone calls, and she was obviously feeling much better.

"Bueno," she answered in a strong but pleasant voice. "How have things gone? What have you got to say?" She probably thought it only proper to use Spanish rather than Nahuat, which would have afforded us at least some privacy. I was limited in what I could tell her or ask her because I knew Doña Carmen and the

other operators in Quetzalan would love nothing better than to tell everyone about these strange telephone calls between a foreigner and a native healer.

After telling me she had taken up trading in the local markets again now that she was feeling better, Rubia asked, "Well, are you going tell me what you saw?"

"Yes, I wrote the dreams all down. Do you want me to read them to you?"

"No, just tell them to me."

I began with the very first dreams, and Rubia didn't say much, commenting only, "Yes," "Go on," or "That's it." She obviously knew Doña Carmen quite well, too. She was obviously unimpressed with these first dreams. "Did you go to that place you went with the chicken?"

"Yes," I replied. The cave had become a motif in several dreams since I had left the Sierra.

"Just tell me those."

I began to recount the dreams where I had seen the cave, and she became much more interested, but her commentaries were not more extensive (perhaps because of Doña Carmen).

When I finished, she said, "Well, you are getting there, though you may not know it. You just keep going there to that place. Next time just tell me about the ones like those last dreams. You'll see, those are the good ones."

We arranged a time to call every week, and Rubia was at the telephone office waiting for my call each time, listening to my dream tales and making only a few cryptic comments. Some weeks were eventful, but others I had nothing to tell her.

After about two months of trying this by phone, Rubia said that I ought to come up to the Sierra to see Inocente too.

August 3, 1976, San Martín Zinacapan,
Sierra de Puebla, Mexico

I WENT UP the following weekend with some of my students from Mexico City. They visited the local markets in Quetzalan and hiked to the incredible waterfalls in the region, while I went to see Rubia and Inocente. I had brought my dream journal, but it proved unnecessary.

Both Rubia and Inocente were waiting for me at Rubia's house when I arrived in San Martín. They had both discussed my dreams and were apparently quite pleased.

After the usual greetings, Inocente began, "He's found it, all right." He asked Rubia, "Did you tell him yet?"

"I couldn't, not on that darned telephone."

Inocente turned to me. "Well, you've been to the four sides of Talocan: the East, the Great Sea; the North, the Cave of the Winds, the Land of the Dead. You've also been to the West, the House of the Women; and the South, the Place of Heat. And there was where you fell into the well."

Inocente was speaking of one of my recent dreams, in which I had again met the enigmatic "Cruz" and fallen with him into a well, then seen a huge and rather terrifying figure with big eyes beckoning me. Cruz restrained me from following the figure and led me out to a path of flowers. I was still trying to figure out who, or what, this curious little man Cruz was. Had I perhaps met him at one time? I had begun asking in the village about the Cruz family.

"When you fell into the well," the old man continued, "that was where you found the heart of it all, the true center of the true Talocan. We didn't know if you could find it, but my *comadre* here said if you kept going to the cave through the Eastern Earth Mouth, you would have to get there.

"In that dream you had right here," he said, motioning to the bench where I had slept in front of Rubia's altar, "you entered from the East and came out from the North. We knew you were on your way through Talocan."

Inocente went on reviewing each dream that I had related to Rubia and recasting it into a description of different journeys into the underworld. What I had thought were some rather nondescript dreams of little real importance rapidly became fantastic tales as the old man told them in a booming Nahuat cadence. Inocente was giving me a lesson in dream interpretation I would never forget, while at the same time describing, in the greatest detail I had ever heard, the form and geography of the underworld—recounting things that I had only read in sixteenth-century chronicles. He could see the world of his ancestors in my dreams, and he was convinced I was seeing it too. Perhaps I was. Perhaps I was just now beginning to recognize it as a world of symbols and traditions open to anyone who would follow the ways of the ancestors.

We talked until late in the evening. When Inocente's son came up to Rubia's house to help his father home, I left too, as I wanted to return to San Martín early the next morning from Quetzalan. Rubia and Inocente wanted me to take offerings to each of the entryways to the underworld, but there wasn't time on this trip—I had to be back in Mexico City for classes on Monday. Before I left, I did agree to take some offerings in the morning to one of the caves near the village. I knew, however, I would be back in San Martín for a week or two before I had to return to the United States.

On the way back from making offerings at a small cave the next morning, I stopped at Inocente's house. As I was leaving he said, "You're as blind down there in the Holy Earth as I am here on the earth. Remember the Lord of the animals? He's the one who will give you eyes for the darkness." I looked at Inocente's clouded old eyes and wondered about what he was saying. "You have to see his animals. They're part of all of us here, and you have to find which ones are yours. You have to find something savage to really do the trick. Then the flower of our ancestors will open up for you. There is going to be a soul raising, and you have to be here for it. Then you'll see."

I really didn't know quite what the old man was talking about, and I asked Rubia on my way out of town. She was rather cagey and said there was a soul that would have to be brought back into the light when I returned, and I would see a lot of things then.

August 18, 1976, San Martín Zinacapan,
Sierra de Puebla, Mexico

It was still the rainy season in the Sierra de Puebla. Mornings were usually brilliant and clear, but the semitropical heat mounted as the sun rose in the sky, and by ten it was becoming almost unbearable. By twelve the clouds began to blot out the merciless sun, and by two each day it would rain. The rains were sometimes torrential, but by five or six o'clock they were usually over. Walking back from the village to Quetzalan each day through the dense, steamy vegetation, past ferns bigger than small trees and dense growths of elephant ears, gave me time and inspiration to think. The rich abundance of the earth burst forth everywhere. The high branches of great trees shading coffee gardens held worlds in themselves of ferns, orchids, bromeliads, and other exotic flora. Often they seemed too heavy for the trees to support. When an occasional branch fell, I would wrest free some of the more unusual orchids and ferns; sometimes I would shinny up trees to capture a rare orchid or strange plant.

I collected the flora of the region the way I collected its folklore and cuisine—to better understand the people, their language, and their world. To me it was all a discovery of worlds I did not know. I had collected scores of stories in the village and was just beginning to understand what it was to be a teller of tales there. Telling a proper tale was still an art form in San Martín, and listening to master narrators perform in the late afternoon or early evening was something to be savored.

When I arrived in the village I usually went straight to Rubia's house for my morning coffee, taking along some sweet bread from Quetzalan, which Rubia loved despite her missing teeth. She gossiped about everyone in the village as she mauled over small bits that she dunked in the coffee. Once in a while she would ask me to recite the prayers I had memorized and show me where to add or take out certain things for certain occasions. She also never tired of talking about her dreams and curings, her work as a midwife, or the miracles of the saints, some of whom were quite novel to me (and, I am sure, the church too). It would still be a few days until everything was ready for the soul raising that I had been asked to help with. We had gone to see the young woman, Maricarmen Sanchez, whose soul Rubia had found in the underworld. It was her *tonal* that was going to be ritually brought into the light.

A soul raising was quite a complicated affair and took some time to arrange. In addition to the bevy of curers who would participate, an entire network of friends, relatives, and ritual kinsmen had to be mobilized to pray for the soul to be freed from the underworld. An entire night would be devoted to prayer and offerings for the earth. The girl would then be taken to the churchyard before dawn and covered with a large cloth. All the participants would intone a long prayer for the light of day, and lifting the cloth as the sun rose, bring both the girl and her soul into the light. The participants then became ritual kinsmen of the girl; they would be protectors of her soul and treated as *compadres* during a huge meal provided by the girl's parents. A soul raising was a great expense. Not only did the meal have to be prepared, but the curers had to be paid and the offerings bought.

At this time I also visited the mountain shrines, caves, pools, waterfalls, and sinkholes where Rubia and Inocente had insisted I leave offerings. These were wondrous places that I would never have found on my own, where nature and the symbolic world converged. Lupe sometimes accompanied me, but as often as not, given directions, I could find these places by myself, hiking through the forests surrounding the village carrying offerings in a shoulder bag.

At one particular mountain shrine, Heart of Sky Mountain, reached by an arduous climb, it was obvious that a huge rock had been the focus of thousands of visits over the centuries. There were broken pieces of old pottery scattered around it. The size of a small house, rivulets of white candle wax had dripped down from every crevice on its face, which had been blackened by perhaps two or three thousand years of copal incense offerings. Not only that, it commanded the most incredible view of the jungles and mountain villages that I had ever seen. From this point the *tepeyolomej* and the *tepehuane,* the "hill hearts" and the "mountain people," could rule over their spectacular domain.

I also visited hidden places. Some were little more than bends in a stream where eddies made pools. Here villagers had left offerings for the *ahuane* and the *alpixque,* the water spirits, for centuries. Others sites were impressive natural wonders like the mountain shrine. I noticed that slowly these wondrous sights were beginning to creep into my own dreams.

The day before the soul raising, a woman had arrived at Rubia's who was obviously from another region. Her dress was that of the

Otomí from near Tenango in the mountains northeast of Quetzalan. Her name was Antonia. Antonia was about Lupe's age, and if it hadn't been for her Otomí costume, they could have been sisters. Two men had also arrived in town from the Totonac region below the village. They were all there to help with the ceremony. I was so involved with my visits to the various shrines around the region, however, that I took little notice of them. The night before the soul raising I went with Rubia to the young woman's house. Her parents, José and Aurelia Sanchez, received us.

"It is darkening, my honored *comadre*, my honored *compadre*," Don José greeted us, though I was by no means a ritual kinsman of his yet. "Come into our humble hovel, and we pray that you give us your holy words of light. We have been awaiting you and the light that you bring."

Rubia replied in an equally formal tone that we were honored to be received into their great house and that we had come to bring their daughter into the light. When we entered there were already many people there, as well as Antonia and the two Totonacs. Offerings were being made and prayers said in a lively atmosphere of smoke, gossip, and conversation. With children crying, the occasional chicken wandering into the house to peck at scraps, and dogs being shooed out, there was the general chaos typical of Nahua ceremonies.

As different individuals went up to the Sanchez altar to pray and make offerings, Rubia sat on a low chair against the far wall opposite the altar, talking and gossiping. She appeared to approve of the arrangements the Sanchez family had made. After a while she turned to me. "Well, you ready with that prayer? You have got to help bring this precious little dove, this little chick, into the light. Put some copal on the fire, and light the two candles I have here for 'them.' Don't forget the tobacco.

"Now don't be too loud," she warned. "You don't want all those 'others' to hear you—just us here and them down there."

Like the villagers, I had already learned to pray in a reverent Nahua mumble. It was far more acceptable than a clearly articulated prayer. Villagers did not raise their voices in prayer but rather lowered them. I nervously began:

Ce huelini titaloc
> You are the one power, Taloc
ce huelini titaloc
> you are the one power, Taloc
ipanin talocan
> in Talocan
ipanin talticpac.
> on the earth . . .

Nican in talocan
> Here in Talocan
nicanin yohualichan
> here in the house of darkness
nimechtatauhtia nen conetzin nen espiritu.
> I beseech you to give me this child, this spirit.
Nican nimechaxcatili ica tantos oraciones
> Here I offer you such prayers
nican nimechtemaktia nofuerza notonal.
> here I let you have all my strength, my soul.
Cani yetoc nejin?
> Where is this one?
cani ancpiaj toconetzin?
> where is our child being kept?
Pox ticonmacazque tehuatzin
> Would you give him to me, O sir

tehuatzin nimitztatautia.
     O sir, I beg of you . . .

When I had finished, I was afforded a position of honor on one of the few Western chairs at the large table in the center of the room, while almost everyone else sat on low benches. I was quite uncomfortable with this arrangement because it was exclusively the Sanchez family at the table. Shots of *refino,* the local white lightning, were beginning to be passed around, and I was sure at this point that I didn't want to stay for the drunk that would ensue.

I went over to Rubia and asked her if it was necessary to stay. No, she said, but I would have to return before dawn. With this, I bid Don José and Doña Aurelia farewell and headed back to Quetzalan. I set my alarm for five in the morning.

The next morning, however, by the time I got out of the hotel and on the path to San Martín it was already approaching six. I walked as fast as I could but was not in time for the actual soul raising. There were still some people, probably with monumental hangovers, mulling around the churchyard, and the huge cloth that had been used to cover the girl was lying on the west side of the plaza. Almost everyone had gone back to the Sanchez house. I went down the hill past the village well to find them. The house was filled with people. A breakfast of coffee, sweet bread, tamales, and *atole,* a corn gruel, was being served, and I was ushered in to the table. Rubia, I was told, had already left. I stayed for some coffee and tamales and then went up to Rubia's house.

Rubia was seated at her altar with her bowl of coffee and some sweet bread as I walked in. I could hear Antonia, the visiting curer, and Lupe in the kitchen.

"Well, you missed it," she said, looking up from her seat, her white hair disheveled and unbraided as if she planned to go back to bed. "You didn't miss much, though. Did Don José feed you?"

"Yes."

"Well, you couldn't see much there anyway. You still don't see much there in Talocan."

"Antonia! Come in here!" she called out to the kitchen in Spanish.

"What do you wish, grandmother?" Antonia came in and stood before us.

"Antonia, how do we see things there in Talocan?"

"Well, we do not see them at all. It is just that other part of us that sees them," Antonia replied.

"I think it is time that this one learned to see with not just his *yollo* and *tonal,* his heart and soul, but all that he has there in the darkness, don't you?" asked Rubia.

"Ah, you mean those savage 'things,' the *naguals?* Perhaps it would be better to get your *compadre* Don Inocente to help Timoteo see with their eyes."

"Perhaps you are right in that. Inocente has a lot of those 'things,' those *naguals*—more than you or I, but maybe that is not a good thing. My *compadre* can do some evil things there in the darkness," Rubia said with finality. Turning away from Antonia and looking at her altar, Rubia said nothing for what seemed a long time. She was considering what Antonia had suggested.

"I think we will go to see Inocente," the old woman said at long last, but in an uncertain voice. "Timoteo, go get some cigarettes, some new ones at Don Pedro's. You'll need them." She asked Antonia, "Can you help me with my hair?"

Rubia had something to discuss and obviously didn't want me around.

When I came back, Rubia was ready to leave for Inocente's, and Antonia was nowhere in sight. Perhaps she and Lupe had gone off to the market, or perhaps Rubia had sent them out on another errand.

I did not know what this old sorceress was planning. After all, I would have thought that she should be down at the Sanchez house, celebrating the return of their daughter's soul and waiting to be paid.

Payment was, after all, a very important part of curing. When Rubia was widowed by her first husband at an early age, the meager fees from the curings she did were all that supported her. Little by little she had amassed enough to start buying and selling small quantities of fruits and vegetables in the local markets. With this and the land that she had managed to buy, she paid for her sons' schooling. Rubia was very astute about making sure her clients paid up quickly, but this time it didn't seem to matter.

As we walked the rutted path to Inocente's house, Rubia started to lecture me. "You know you have to be careful of my *compadre*. This little old man has done some evil deeds. He was a *pistolero*, a real killer. He's a man of great knowledge, but you have to keep a close watch on him, too. He can be two-faced and foul. He seems to like you, but if he thinks that you're a threat, be very careful. He doesn't use a pistol any more, but he can snuff out your candle in nothing flat."

Though I had still never mentioned the tape to anyone, I thought about it again. "I know, grandmother, that your *compadre* has quite a history and he's a dangerous man, but why would he come after me?"

"Never tell him more than he is willing to tell you. Never let him know who you really see there in Talocan. Never let the old man fool you. He may be almost blind in this world, but he sees everything in the world of night. There, his eyes are clearer than yours or mine. He's like an eagle that can soar high in the sky hunting for a little dove or a rabbit. If he attacks, you're as good as dead. His bite is worse than the viper's. He'll help you to see there in

Talocan, but he'll want to use your eyes too, so be very careful about what you tell the old man, you hear!

"Inocente knows the ways of a hundred savage things there in Talocan. He can be lion. He can be tiger. He can be an eater of men, a wolf, a horse, a snake, a dog, a lizard, a vulture, or an eagle. He can show you the ways of all of them. I know some of these things but not all of them. I want you to help me! I cannot do it by myself. We need him. He's a very powerful man. Tell my *compadre* half of what he asks, and tell him nothing else," she insisted.

Now we were just turning down the path to Inocente's house, and as we entered, Rubia's tone changed. "The light is upon us, my honored *compadre*. We greet you in the light of the day."

"Enter and seat yourselves," replied Inocente. "What brings you here after the soul raising, did it not go well?" He sat down at his regular place and motioned us to be seated next to him in front of the altar.

"It went very well. The little one is back with us; the little dove is flying about her parent's house now," said Rubia. "What brings us here is this one, the tree man, Timoteo. He still doesn't see well in the world of darkness, and he cannot speak. He has not found that other part of him that will let him go freely about the world of night."

"Ah, the animal that is his down there, that he shares his life with, his *nagual,*" Inocente replied. "Have you seen it, Rubia? I have not. Perhaps it is that cow, or bull, that he saw."

"No, I doubt that. The bull was surely one of 'them' chasing his soul about in dreams."

"Has he seen any animals there?" Inocente asked.

"No, not that he has mentioned," Rubia replied.

Inocente turned to me and asked, "Well, Timoteo, did you see any animals there in the dreams?"

"No," I replied, "the only thing I saw was that man."

"'Cruz.' Hmmm," said Inocente, "you told us before about him. What did he look like?"

I could feel Rubia's icy stare and remembered Inocente's warning months ago, as well as Rubia's more recent one. What could I say?

"Come on, what did he say, and have you seen him again?" Inocente asked.

I didn't answer.

"Well, 'Cruz' can't help him to see and to get about there anyway, so what are you so interested for?" Rubia interjected.

"No reason, just thought it might help us find his animal," replied Inocente wryly.

"What he has to find now is his *nagual,* the true one that he shares his life with. Cruz may be able to help him later. He may be able to show him things there in the darkness, but he needs that animal to roam freely in the world of night," Rubia insisted. "Your *nagual* is your eyes, your ears," she explained to me, "your feet and your wings there in the world of night. Without it, you are just taken there in the darkness, and you fall where you may. If you really want to find your way about in the night, it is the *nagual* that must show you. You must become the *nagual.* You have to dream of the *nagual,* and then you have to find it." She paused. "Have there been no dreams with animals, not even little ones?"

"None that I could remember." The two old sages began to push and probe me about animals, but unfortunately there was still nothing I could tell them.

Inocente then asked me, "When you go from place to place in Talocan, do you fly, do you walk, or what?"

I didn't know.

"Do you look down at things, or up at them?"

"Well, down at them," I said.

"Like from the trees?" Inocente asked with a glint of a smile. "Maybe it is something that lives in the trees," he said to Rubia.

They both began questioning me about animals that lived in trees, such as birds and squirrels.

"Was it a monkey?" Inocente asked Rubia. They both thought that would be appropriate, but I told them that I had never seen a monkey in dreams, and in fact I hadn't.

"Maybe it's a *mapache,* then," suggested Inocente. A *mapache* is a raccoonlike creature with a banded tail.

"Maybe it was a *mapache,*" I said.

"Well, then you have to find the *mapache,* and if he comes to you in dreams, then you know that he is your *nagual,*" Inocente said. "Lucas is taking me to the *cafetal* tomorrow to cut the brush from around the coffee bushes. You can come with us if you want, and maybe you will see something there. There are *mapaches* out there."

I hoped that Lucas would not be displeased with Inocente's offer, as he was going there to work. I went out to the front of the house where he was stacking wood while Inocente and Rubia remained, discussing my *nagual.*

Everything seemed agreeable, so we arranged to leave for the *cafetal* the next morning before dawn, and I went back to Quetzalan to get my things. I returned that evening and slept on a bench at Inocente's. Before dawn I was up helping Lucas and his wife with the horses, and we were off. Old Inocente rode a gray, swayback mule, but I preferred walking. Just before midday we arrived, and Lucas's wife set about cleaning out the lean-to that we would stay in and starting a fire. We had coffee and *gorditas,* corn dough stuffed with bean paste toasted on the *comal,* and then Inocente began one of his long tales. As always, he was a master narrator, and it was wonderful to listen to him through the rainy afternoon.

The rains stopped just before dusk, as Inocente finished telling of a man who was caught in the forest and became an animal. He asked Lucas if a *mapache* lived anyplace around there, then he sent Lucas out with me to see if we could find the animal. We walked through the forest with our eyes on the treetops until it was almost dark, but we didn't see anything. Finally near a small stream Lucas pointed to a tree. I took out my binoculars, and sure enough, there was a striped tail there, the *mapache*. We didn't want to disturb it, so we returned.

When we got back, Inocente asked, "You find that thing?"

"We did," Lucas told him, and Inocente then began explaining to me just what I would have to do. I would have to watch the *mapache* to see if it came to me in my dreams. We decided that the next morning Lucas would help me set up a camp near where we had seen the animal. It was a beautiful spot, and a couple of days out there sounded perfect to me.

For three days I tried to keep track of the *mapache*, follow its tracks along the stream and see what it ate: crawfish, prawns, small fish, fruit, and various kinds of eggshells. There was one tree it slept in almost all day, and at night I really couldn't follow it. On the third day, thinking I would be sure to find the thing and follow it in its nightly wanderings, I dozed under the tree in which it slept, but that evening I never saw it come down and never saw it again. I had probably scared it off.

Meanwhile, as I sat waiting for the *mapache,* a *tlacuache,* a possum, raided my camp, dumping my one cooking pot and leaving its characteristic unpleasant odor everywhere. The tracks were unmistakable.

I went to see Inocente the next morning to tell him the *mapache* had gone and mentioned the possum's raid on my cooking gear.

"Maybe that's your *nagual* looking for you." Inocente sounded delighted, and told me I had to go back to find the possum, but the group was returning the next morning to the village. Lucas had finished cutting the underbrush, and the whole area seemed more like a well-cultivated garden now than the brambly patch of forest that I had first seen. His work was done until the coffee harvest began. We all sat under the lean-to as the afternoon rain began again. The old man told several tales of the exploits of the possum and told me I would have to go back to look again at dusk. That was the time that it came out from the cave. Lucas's wife gave me some *gorditas* and beans to take back to my camp.

Back at my campsite, I started a small fire and put the *comal*, the griddle, over it, saying Lupe's prayer to the fire dogs and heating up the *gorditas*. I gave a few crumbs to the flames and left a few out for the possum. I was back on the schedule of the mountains, sleeping with the sunset and awakening just before dawn. When I awoke, I could tell from the scent in the air that the possum had been there again. I followed its tracks with my flashlight into the brambles and saw the possum sleeping in a tree. It barely moved all day, and when I returned to camp I left some more food out for it. That night I kept the fire at a low glow and waited.

The possum returned and rummaged about near the fire. It was said through much of Mesoamerica that this animal had stolen the fire from the gods, lighting its tail and fleeing with the flame. The possum rutted around my camp for several hours and returned to the same tree at dawn. I followed it.

All morning until the rains came, I watched the possum sleeping, then I went back to camp for a nap. The possum did come down to me in my dream. This was what Inocente had told me I should see. I decided to wait another day or so before returning to the village and instead patiently watch the possum and enjoy my stay in the forest.

When I finally packed up my gear and hiked up to Inocente's house in town, I had seen the possum twice more in my dreams. It was becoming an anthropomorphic figure, and like the shrines, it was something I was beginning to see regularly. It is strange to be told you would see certain things in a dream state and then see them. I had always thought of dreaming as a will-less state, if I had thought about it at all. Inocente had said I would get an animal companion and now I had one. A *doppelgänger?* Would I soon be able to control my dreams the way Rubia and Inocente seemed to? When I arrived in San Martín, I went to Inocente's and told the old man what had happened. He was pleased.

"Well, now you have seen it, but seeing is not enough. You have to have it, so that you can call it out whenever you need it. That possum is your eyes and your feet there in the world of dreams. You have to be able to call him out when you need him." I was surprised.

Inocente sent me back to the forest with Lucas that afternoon, and we prepared a trap for the animal. Near the fire we dug a two-foot pit and put out a can with some sardines for bait. Once the possum stuck its head in the can it would be caught, and that night we got it. Lucas dispatched the beast quickly, and we skinned it, stretching the skin out on sticks. We smoked the meat on skewers over the fire most of the next day, protecting the fire from the rain with a lean-to of branches. By dusk we were on our way back to Inocente's.

He was up waiting for us when we got to the house.

"Well, you got it," he said. The aroma of the smoked meat was all over us.

"Sure did, Pop," Lucas answered. "We even smoked it. Should be enough for a few tacos."

"Go ask Elena to heat up some tortillas," Inocente told his son. Turning to me, he said, "Now that you have the possum, you have to know about it." Lucas brought in some tacos made from the possum and a hot sauce of freshly toasted red chilies. As we sat casually eating, Inocente went into a tale of the possum I had heard before. It felt a bit strange eating my own *nagual,* so I interrupted Inocente and asked him if it was all right to eat the possum.

"Sure is," he replied, "and tasty too. It'll make you strong and virile."

"You can eat your own *nagual?*" I asked.

"Sure. That's not your *nagual,* maybe it is one of its sisters or brothers, but your *nagual* is safe with the Lord of the animals in the cave where he protects them. Why, if that had been yours, you wouldn't be here. You share the *tonal,* life, and have the same heart. When he dies, you do too."

"Is this someone else's *nagual?*" I asked, looking at the half-charred meat. Inocente left this question unanswered. Instead, he broke into another tale of how a man had been tricked by a witch into killing his own *nagual* and died with the animal in the same trap. Lucas retired to the cookhouse with his wife and went to sleep, but Inocente just kept on spinning his tales for me. Finally, the old man finished.

"You going to go back to Quetzalan tonight?" he asked me.

"Yes," I said, "I think I will."

"Well, you know your *tlacuache* will protect you," exclaimed the old man.

"How?" I asked.

"You see this?" he said, pointing to the long, thin drying tail. "When it is good and hard it'll take out an eye like that!" He made a sinister gesture. "Right through the eye and poff! you put someone's lights out for good. You have to hold the thing like this in your hand, and when someone is close, right there is where you put it," he said, pointing at a spot at the corner of the eye.

"You put it in fast and leave it there a minute, and their lights are out for good. When you pull it out, be sure you don't pull the eye out. It goes straight to the soft stuff. No one can tell what happened.

"The pouch is good for putting someone's lights out too. You put the seeds of the flower we call the yellow wax flower in it and mix in some copal, then put it covered on the altar for three days. Give it to someone with the copal to burn, or roll a bit of the mixture in a cigarette. One whiff of that smoke, and they're gone. They can't breathe, and they suffocate 'in the pouch.' Your victim is what we call 'tucked away in the possum's pouch.'"

"Aren't those things witches do?" I asked, trying to sound as naive as possible.

"Yes, but you have to know how to do them too, or they are going to get you. Every *nagual* has some good things and a bit of evil. You have to know both."

"You can have more than one *nagual?*"

"Of course," he replied. "Look here!" He reached under the altar near where he was seated and pulled out a plaited reed box about a foot and a half long and a few inches high.

In the dim light of the candles on the altar he opened the box. It was filled with bones, beaks, and other parts of different animals. There were also some dried dark seeds and a copal bag.

"This one is my bat. I got him a long time ago," he said with a glint in his eye, holding up a piece of dried bat wing. "This little thing has protected me for many years against the witches—helped me get rid of a few of them, too. This one is my night bird." He held up a piece of a beak. "There are things he can do that will sure put out someone's lights fast."

"All those are your *naguals?*" I asked. Inocente had dozens of pieces of bones, necks, wings, and skins of various animals stored in his box.

"Sure are," the old man said, holding up some large canine teeth. "These are some of the best ones. This is a coyote, and this is my tiger." He was holding a large cat's claw.

"I thought we only had one *nagual* in the underworld."

"No, no, no," the old man replied. "There is one *nagual* that is yours, but when you travel in the night in the land of darkness you need many of them to protect you and to take your place in the cave. All you have to do is put this or that little bit of the *nagual* on the altar, and it will come to you in a dream. Then it will take you where you want to go in Talocan, and if you wish to speak to the Lords or the 'others' of Talocan, your *nagual* can do that for you. You cannot speak to the Lords face-to-face. You need the *nagual* to get around in the underworld. We are born with just one animal, but you can find dozens of them when you need them—that's right, dozens and dozens of them."

"How?" I asked.

"Well, first you have to find the animal, and you have to see it; then you have to get it. Someone who knows its ways can tell you what it does in the realm of darkness, where it goes and how it gets there. These things are our eyes, our feet, our voices, our protectors and patrons in the night. You can go from one to another, first being a *tigre,* then a mouse, slipping in and out of different places there in the darkness. They can speak to those 'others,' the ones in the cave, too. Those others see just the animal and don't know it is you speaking. You can ask them for lost souls, gold, or whatever, that way.

"Our brothers and sisters, the *curanderos,* know the ways of these 'things' of the night; I can tell you about them, so can Rubia, but there are others too. If you follow the 'good path,' you need a lot of help from these animals, and it is better to have big strong ones, but the doves and mice can be useful too. They can scurry into little places under cover," he laughed. "You need them all. This possum is just the first one, and maybe he is not your real brother. Maybe he is not your 'other.' Maybe you do not share the soul of this animal, but he will help you find which one does.

"There are those who change to other forms to do evil—those are the witches—but you do not have to do anything evil to shift to other forms in the underworld. There is much evil that can be done with these things. Take my *tigre,*" he said, showing me a pair of leather tubes about three inches long with two large canine teeth mounted on their ends. "He kills with his teeth right here." He pointed to the lower part of his jugular vein and made a ripping motion across his leathery neck. "They're done!

"Then there is the bat. When he hangs, he embraces himself. When you embrace someone like that, right here," he went on, pointing to a particular spot near the nape of the neck and putting his arms out in a mockery of an embrace, "push hard there, and it snaps. Then they are gone. Their candle is snuffed out."

Inocente went on describing not only other dastardly methods of murder, some of which I didn't dare let on that I already knew of, but also the good points of the *naguals* he had acquired over the years. Some could dig a hole quickly to escape from a witch, he told me; others could hide easily in the world of darkness.

I was fascinated. The list went on and on. Even when I heard things the second and third time, I didn't stop him. I didn't want to break the narration.

Finally we both tired, and I left for Quetzalan. When I woke the night porter and got to my room, it was well past midnight, but all I could think about was this murderous old gentleman. I had to see Rubia first thing in the morning, I knew that.

ON THE WAY out of Quetzalan I bought sweet rolls for Rubia, her favorite kind, and I arrived at her house at just about the usual time for coffee. She was not at all surprised to see me.

"Well, what did you find?" she asked me before I even sat down and took out the rolls.

"It wasn't the *mapache,* but a possum, and I have it here in my bag," I replied. I had taken the tail and the pouch from Inocente's house last night.

"Well, let's see it," she said, after a minute.

I took the rolls and then the pieces of the *tlacuache,* wrapped in plastic, out of my bag.

"We have to dry the tail like this," she said straightening it out. "I'll show you how we do it. Did Inocente tell you how to use it?"

"Like that?" I replied with a gesture to the point on the inside corner of the eye, the way that Inocente had shown me.

"Right, I thought he'd show you that. These things are our ears, our eyes, our feet, and our wings in the darkness. They are good, but there is something savage to each of them, just as there is something savage in each of us. They are the wild part of the soul that we all have, and they protect us against the evils that can be done in the darkness. If you ask the Lords of darkness for justice, you can use these things. If a witch attacks you, or if someone does evil to you, or one of yours, you can use them. Witches use them all the time, but they all get it in the end for their evil ways. If it is not justice the witches seek from the Lords, the Lords will get angry, and they are done for. You can't use these things—they will not work—unless you seek 'their' permission, unless you are in their favor, and unless you do their will."

"You have these things too?" I asked Rubia.

"Sure, we all have them, but you can't use them except to get around and help souls in the darkness, unless you have their permission. 'They' will only grant permission if your cause is just, if you help them find justice here on the earth."

"Let me see your box of these things," I asked.

"It's not here," Rubia said evasively.

"Where is it?"

"It's not right here, but if you really want to see it, I can get it."

"Yes, please get it." I wanted to see what this grandmotherly sorceress had in her bag of tricks.

We went out together to the back of the house, and in the rafters of an old thatched shed was a reed box just like the one Inocente had shown me the night before. We brought it into the house and set it down on Rubia's altar.

"Lupe, will you go get Don Inocente?" she called out to her daughter-in-law.

As soon as the door was closed, we barred it, and then Rubia opened her reed box. Inside, wrapped in an embroidered cloth, were the same dozens of patches of fur, buzzard beaks, and claws from different animals, but there were also some flakes of obsidian and potsherds that I hadn't seen in Inocente's bag. I asked her about those objects first, and she told me they were from the ancestors and that they would help me see and talk with those who still lived in the world of darkness.

"Maybe one of these will help you find your friend 'Cruz' there in the darkness. Never mind what Inocente says, this Cruz may be very helpful to you. Inocente may just be afraid of him. Maybe he is waiting there in the darkness for my *compadre*. Put this," she said, pointing to the small obsidian blade, "with the stones on your altar, and then you will be able to see him. It is from our ancestors, all those who have gone before us, and it is made from the 'black hill heart stone.' You will use it to see the 'hill hearts' too. You will need more *naguals* to find Cruz unless he is looking for you. That's not good if he's looking for you. He could be an unsatisfied soul who still seeks justice. Trust where the *naguals* take you, but beware of what this Cruz asks."

Was this bit of obsidian part of a blade from her ancestors? Why did she think it would help me to "call out" Cruz? If he came of his own free will, that was trouble, she said. If I found him there in my dreams, that was all right. Was this a way to control my own dreaming? Was the "witch" a metaphor for the uncontrolled, the "wild" element? The unconscious? I thought of Freud, of course, and Jung, and of the matter of witchcraft in the sixteenth century, but that was all too simple. The Western explanations of psychology did not fit this Aztec tradition. What would Freud's dreams have looked like to his patients?

Rubia interrupted these thoughts. "The *naguals,* once you have them, are always yours. They are part of you. Someone who knows the road of the ancestors has to explain each new one to you, but they are your own and will always help you. Take the *tzopelote* here," she said, holding up a buzzard's beak. "This *tzopelote* eats the dead, but he is also my eyes there in the darkness, and he can see the dead before 'they' can, there in the darkness. I can find who I want before they are consumed by the 'others,' who are not our brothers."

Rubia went on explaining each of the items in her reed box to me until Inocente arrived. When Lupe knocked at the door, Rubia quickly hid all the things from her box and put it behind her. She was taking no chance that Inocente would see anything. I opened the door to let them in. Inocente looked uncomfortable, as he usually was in someone else's home.

"Well, have you been telling Timoteo about *naguals?*" he asked.

"Yes, a few things at least. Now I think we both have to tell him where they go and how we use them."

"She has been showing you her *naguals?*" the old man asked me.

"Yes," I replied, and Rubia's stare made it clear that she didn't want me talking about them.

"She has more than I do?" he asked.

"Nearly the same amount," I replied.

"She's got *tigres* and 'people eaters' in there?" he prodded.

"Yes, I think so. Well, maybe," I said vaguely.

Inocente was fishing around for more information but saw quickly he wouldn't get it from me. He would have loved to know just what animals Rubia had acquired. The dynamics of this little triangle were becoming rather frustrating, and I figured that it could only get worse.

We spent the rest of the morning talking about *naguals* and what they did. There were numerous other techniques of dispatching a witch or an enemy. Most all of them were nearly undetectable and murderous, but Rubia and Inocente also told me much about the characteristics of the different animals and their position in the underworld, where they could go and what they could do there. It was quite a lesson in the ways of the ancestors and their world and gave me a much clearer picture, too. I was beginning to understand how curing became killing in the Aztec way.

I agreed to help Inocente home around midday, and before leaving, both old practitioners told me to be sure never to tell anyone else what we had discussed. That would surely lay me open to charges of witchcraft in the village. This was something that only those adept in the ways of dreams should know.

With what they had told me, I could see why few except the initiated should know these things. This was a highly specialized and esoteric type of knowledge open only to practitioners. I was beginning to see how all this worked. I was finally weaving together the disparate threads of their world.

As I left Inocente at his house, he told me, "Now you are prepared to see in the darkness. Follow the path, and you will see that the ancestors are here. Their path is the 'good path.'"

Chapter 6

THE WITCH

Three months later. January 14, 1977,
Quetzalan, Puebla, Mexico

THE RICH SMELL OF ROASTING COFFEE
WOKE ME FROM ONE
OF THE MOST SPECTACULAR DREAMS
I'd had since I'd begun
to follow "the path."
Don Ismael was slowly turning his old wood-fired roaster

under the eaves across the street. The weather was damp and cold. It had been raining steadily for almost three days. This was one of the fearsome *Nortes,* or northern winds, that occasionally engulfs the Sierra in winter. The Nortes are the cause of much sickness and suffering in the villages, especially for those who live in thatched huts with flimsy walls of sticks daubed with mud. Even my hotel room was cold and damp, and I had not ventured out much, nor had I been to San Martín in three days.

I was still foggy and confused from sleep but knew that I had to set this epic down in my dream journal. As I began to collect my thoughts, I realized, perhaps for the first time, that I was finally beginning to look at my dreams the way Rubia and Inocente did. I knew the entries and exits they had taught me to find in dreams and the animals that I could enter and travel with. I recognized the cities, the towns, and the sacred places of the underworld. I was beginning to know the world of darkness as a part of everyday life.

I was accepting the reality of the things I was taught to see in dreams. I was learning to interpret selectively and to edit my dreams and dream tales when I told them.

I sat down at the rickety table with my journal, looking up at the gray sky and then out through the drizzling rain at the ancient cobblestone streets and decaying buildings of Quetzalan. Closing my eyes again, I could see Talocan before me. I was back in the world of dreams. It was a world of images I had never expected to see or understand. As I wrote, the images became more vivid and real.

I ENTERED TALOCAN through the Great Eastern entryway, that huge mouth of the earth with viny teeth where I had sacrificed the chicken. The sociable bats were there on the ceiling of the cave conversing and chirping. I talked with them for a while and saw them guarding their children. The bats and the bat people are very helpful in the world of night. They see everything and can travel quickly from one part of Talocan to another. They had told me nothing of import, but as I took off into the darkness, one of their children chirped out, "There's a witch in there!" I took little heed of what the bat child had said as I flew on through the night.

I had never had a confrontation with a witch and hoped that I never would. Though Inocente and Rubia had told me much about their ways, I did not yet fully understand what a witch was. A witch was someone who did evil deeds, a shape shifter in the world of dreams. It was someone who sought harm for others, a menacing figure who turned good into evil and dreams to nightmares and sometimes killed people. That was all I understood about witches.

I flew on through the night over forests and mountains. It was like looking out of the window of my father's plane when I was a child. There were fields and streams; the landscape had that peculiar Midwestern look of great flat squares, a patchwork of earth, a checkerboard of field and forest, not at all like the mountains of Mexico.

The greens and golds underneath me were a blur of color, and finally I found myself in a high treetop, sitting on a branch watching what went on below me. The *tlacuache* was there. He had become a regular figure in my dreams, sitting up and taking on an almost human form. He would rarely speak to me, but his mouth was moving as if he were speaking. I went with the *tlacuache*. I took on that form—that is what the two old sages would have said. I became the *tlacuache* and crawled down the tree.

There were large, craggy rocks all around, black and covered with brush. It was rather like the Pedregal, the barren volcanic waste on the edge of Mexico City where the National University was built. There was a constant echo, perhaps of voices, as I moved through the black rocks and brush. On the ground I was in a maze. All around me the rocks folded over themselves, with sharp spines of cacti and agaves protruding from every crevice. There were voices sounding half-familiar and almost recognizable, though I couldn't hear what they were saying.

As I came around the edge of a large outcrop, there were ten or twenty people seated at a large conference table. It was a dark Spanish table like those in the refectories of early monasteries, but I did not know the people. They were dressed in native garb, suits, *guyaberas,* and leather jackets, the kinds of clothes my colleagues wore at the institute, but I could not see any of their faces. There was obviously an extraordinary debate going on, but I could not understand the words. It was all an incoherent babble to me, yet everyone was gesturing wildly.

As I sat and watched, the faces became clearer to me, but they were those of animals. I could recognize some by the way they were dressed. They were my fellow anthropologists. Juan, at the head of the table, was a great old bear presiding over the whole affair, and Alfonso, a great dark eagle or hawk with a balding pate and a stained white *guyabera,* was ready to swoop down on anyone who misplaced a word. Olivia had become a grandmotherly old shrew in bright native garb with jingling jewelry who jumped into the fray, staring her opponents down with her black eyes. Marta was a gray, old *tlacuache* with a dowdy dress who peered over her bifocals, taking constant notes. José Luis was a black-and-white bird in a suit, his characteristic glasses perched on the edge of his long beak, about to fall off. He spoke in precise and studied words, and everyone stopped to listen. Every once in a while he would spread his wings for effect. All of them were shouting at once in an incessant babble.

Finally, Don Leopoldo walked up to the table and began to speak. He read from notes, wearing the rumpled suit that was his trademark, with his long hair swept back over his collar. I could see his whiskers twitching and the protruding teeth of a rodent under that long snout—he was a great rat, or mouse, with huge round ears. He was speaking in a clear and elegant Spanish that I could understand, even though none of what he was saying made any sense at all. Everyone at the conference table listened intently as the speech droned on.

A huge, fat, old gray cat went up to the table and quietly purred, also in elegant Spanish, "This is enough, Don Leopoldo. Shall we have him here or not?"

This gray cat was so huge that he couldn't stand, but rather squatted behind Leopoldo in a wide chair with his two fat legs hanging down. It was obviously Don Arturo, one of the great old men who presided over his offices and libraries this way in approving silence.

"We shall have him," the unkempt gray rodent replied, and the conversation then broke into an unintelligible babble again with everyone congratulating one another with handshakes and *abrazos.*

There was suddenly a cold, wet breeze and the smell of mildew everywhere. Perhaps I had partially awakened and was feeling the dampness of my room there in the night, but at that point in the dream everything began to change. Everything became dark, and the babble and chaos became the frightened sounds of animals scurrying for cover. A scabious street dog standing up in a skirt began to bark at Leopoldo, then it turned and began barking at me. Its voice was shrill and vicious. Its front feet pawed at me.

The meeting was receding from view, and I was beginning to run. Then I saw it behind me: a huge gray woman in a brown suit with a bristly bouffant hairdo that looked as though it was made from dried corn husks. She had great black eyes and gold jewelry everywhere that seemed to be burning and a long ratlike snout with whiskers, which were covered by layer upon layer of ghastly green makeup. Her mouth opened like a toad's, and the huge tongue shot out at me. It stuck on the rocks, and she reeled it back in like a whip. Again she spat that prehensile tongue out at me, and, splot! it caught on the rocks right next to me.

I was trying to flee, and the rocks were beginning to give way to trees. There were at first great black trees, ancient ones, as in the pristine forests of the Pacific coast of Oaxaca. The ancient trees were covered with lichens and moss. The area looked primeval. As I ran, the tongue would land in front of me, splat! again, and return with the crack of a whip.

This was what a witch was.

I whirled through the trees of the great Oaxacan forest and tumbled into a stream, but the woman with the toad's mouth kept on pursuing me there in the darkness. I was swirling, tossing and tumbling, unable to escape, unable to awaken.

An arm reached out from the chaos for me. I could not see whose at first. The whirling and tumbling suddenly subsided, and I found myself on a large sandy riverbank. "Cruz" was there, the little man with the kiss-me-quick mustache and long, swept-back black hair. He was holding on to me as I looked up into his bright, deep-brown eyes.

"Come on! Let's go!" he said to me in Nahuat, pulling me up with his hand around my waist.

I was still dizzy and stumbled back down into the sandy ground, but Cruz helped me up once more.

"She almost got you there, that one did. We have to go, or she'll get us both. Come on!" he insisted.

Cruz stood out against the dark sand in his white poplin shirt and *calzones* tied twice around the waist. His *huaraches* were sandals of heavy white leather straps with black soles made from automobile tires. His dress was typical of the region and impeccably correct.

"There's an old *tlacuache* who lives over there at the side of the river," he said. "We'll see if she will hide us in there until that witch goes by."

He took me to a small hole, and we both shrank down until we entered it. There was a feeling of falling over as my hands became clawed feet. Once inside I could see that we were both *tlacuaches* in there. Cruz's white clothing became thick white fur, and I could feel my beard growing and engulfing me in long gray hair. There was another *tlacuache* there, and Cruz spoke to her. She had long gray hair and a grandmotherly smile that reminded me of Rubia.

"O, our honored grandmother, will you keep us, will you protect us here? There is a witch that seeks this companion, this man, who searches for us out there in the darkness, in the fog."

"Yes, my sons, seat yourselves here. Wait, and then you must escape. You must take this one, the one who still has his flesh, out of the darkness," she said. She was now an old woman in neat traditional dress, her head piled high with the knotted purple and green strands of her *mecapal.*

While we waited, Cruz and the old woman talked. She told him that we must find the Cave of the Winds and the Land of the Dead in the North if I was to escape. Finally, I could feel the witch that had been following us go by in a great storm of fury above the entrance to our hole. Cruz and I were two scared, small animals trembling and hiding from a vicious predator. I could feel her searching and remained silent. The old woman looked scared. I was petrified.

Finally the feeling the witch was near passed, and I relaxed. Cruz bid the old woman farewell and promised that I would bring her things from the world of light. Standing up, we grew taller and emerged from the hole. It was dark, but everything seemed very clear.

"Now we must fly," Cruz told me, and suddenly we were both turning into the dark, mottled whippoorwills that come out at dusk in the Sierra. We flew up and sat on a branch. He whispered softly into my ear with a windy voice.

"Lhhhet'sssss gohhhh!"

We both flew over villages and towns there in the dream. I followed the bird through the darkness. Finally we landed in another great tree. Looking down, we could hear voices and see men in native garb clearing brush, as Lucas had done in his *cafetal,* cutting trees and carrying wood.

"These are the *kiyauhtiomej,*" Cruz told me. "They are gathering wood for the fires in the Cave of the Winds. We will follow them there to the cave, and you can find your way out into the light."

We watched them carefully cutting, chopping, stacking, and loading wood for some time. They looked like any other villagers hard at work. They could have been the medieval burghers of Brueghel but for their dress.

Cruz sat with me and watched. We talked, but I do not remember what we spoke about. I felt an immediate liking for my companion in this dream. He was no longer an enigmatic figure and seemed to be the part of me that kept things clear and in perspective. Cruz was a dark, muscular, tight-skinned man with a compassionate way about him that I immediately admired. We sat in the tree a long time watching these supernatural Aztecs at work.

Finally Cruz said to me. "Come on! They are going. Find your *tlacuache,* and we'll follow them through the trees."

Cruz had already become a *tlacuache* with smooth white fur again. I saw another *tlacuache* with heavy gray fur, and there I was again scurrying along the branches and dancing across the limbs. I followed Cruz, leaping through the trees. We were like two children at play as we followed the men with huge loads of firewood on their backs. They marched in single file. Their huffing, puffing, and groaning under the weight of their loads sounded like a dirge.

Entering a deep, dark hole in the brush like a black line of ants, they all disappeared.

"That's it," said Cruz. "That's the entry to Miquitalan, the Land of the Dead. The Lords and Ladies of death live there and rule with their minions, the *talocanca* and the *mictiani*. 'They' eat the flesh of the dead—and the living, too, if they can find them," he said, giving me a knowing glance. "The dead are brought here. Their bones are stripped, and they become a *tonal,* like me. But the Cave of the Winds is beyond this palace of death. We must slip past 'them' and find our way out of there. We have to find the cave where the Lord and the Lady of the winds live, and we must be very careful not to wander into these palaces of death. We might become like the Lord and Lady of death."

What kept him from being devoured in this darkness? Who was this man? Was he, as Rubia had said, someone who had lived in the village, or at least on the earth with men and women?

We climbed down from the trees and crawled into the hole where the peasants, the *kiyauhtiomej,* the "lightning bolt ones," had disappeared. It was pitch black, and all I could hear was Cruz telling me, "Shhh! you don't want them to hear. They are eaters of flesh here. Follow me.

"Now be careful. Let me look ahead and be sure that this is not the way to the Land of the Dead. They do not seek you yet, but if they saw you, they might just strip you down to your bones, and then you'd be lost in the darkness. You could never come out into the light again." Cruz went on ahead and came back shortly.

"It's this way," he said. "I found the kitchens of the Cave of the Winds. They are here, the big pots that hold the tempests' clouds, rain, and lightning bolts."

It was true. We were in a huge kitchen with great pots bubbling on the fires at one end of the room and a long table in the center. It even smelled good. On the far side of the room there were three huge, clay bean pots all neatly covered with wooden tops. These had been described to me many times in tales. They contained the clouds, winds, and rain. Cruz pointed out in the corner the *metate* used by the toad woman, the grinder of corn for the Lords of the winds and waters.

There was no one here, though, and we passed freely from room to room in the cave. There was a constant sound of wind and rain in the cave like an unrelenting storm. We heard movement, and Cruz motioned me back as he went on ahead again.

Returning, he said, "That's it, they all are with the Lords of this place. All of them are there: the lightning ones, the water ones, the wind ones, and the smoke ones. They're with the Lords, sitting on great thrones in the cave. They must be making some kind of big storm or planning something foul together." Cruz pointed to my right and said, "We can go out through here where the waters come from."

We went on, and the sounds of rain and rushing water were everywhere. Finally we came to a great cavern with a waterfall and a pool from which rushed a huge river.

"This is where they pour out the waters for the world of light," Cruz told me. "The lakes, the streams, and the rivers all come from here."

The cold was damp and bone chilling. Cruz helped me over the rocks and stones in the path, and things began to become brighter. The light turned to an almost silver dawn. We arrived at last at one of the entrances to the cave that looked out onto the entire Sierra. We could see the mountains through the patchy fog. We were looking down at the valleys below.

"I can go no farther," Cruz said. "You take the night bird and fly off to the light, and you will be well, but take care that none of those 'others' follow you there. The witch is yours to deal with, and she must be stopped or she will do you harm. If you live a good life, they cannot get you. Now fly before that witch comes after you. Remember that she is still looking for you."

With that, Cruz disappeared, and I woke from my long dream.

I FINISHED THE journal, put it aside, and looked around the room. I found that if I wrote before I thought and before I even had coffee, I could retain the essences of these strange dreams. I was seeing and experiencing things I never thought possible. Since my search for Rubia's bewitched soul, had I changed the way I looked at my own soul and traditions? The dreams and the way I was being taught to interpret dreams had merged, and I was being swept along by my constant immersion in the world that lay beyond Rubia's and Inocente's closed eyes. I was becoming a curer, a dreamer, and a shaman. In many cultures it was still considered dangerous to ignore the callings of the gods. Who were all these ancient gods? How much was I really in control of myself now, and how much was I obliged to a tradition that I did not even yet fully understand?

Most might think I had gone too far for credible anthropology, but for me, this was what anthropology was all about. The research I was doing at the National University was strictly linguistic at the time, and this type of ethnology was a sideline. Fernando Horcasitas, Doris Heyden, and Thelma Sullivan were some of the few colleagues that I confided in about the situation, and they all encouraged me in my work in the Sierra. Even with these close friends, however, I was very careful about what I said, especially about the dreams and where I went in them.

The rain had slowed, but a cold, grayish mist covered everything. I thought about the cemetery that I passed on every trip to San Martín. It was perched on a hill where the road bent.

Why did "Cruz" appear in my dreams? Did "he" perhaps lie up there in an unmarked grave? Had he been the subject of a long-forgotten conversation? Although it would take months, I resolved to someday see if he really existed by checking the town archives—a rat's nest of old papers stored in the moldering town hall that now housed the weaver's cooperative. I left my room, drank some coffee, bought some sweet bread, and trudged off through the fog and damp to find Rubia.

I was still wondering about Cruz when I arrived at Rubia's house.

"Good afternoon, the darkness approaches," I called out.

"There you are," Lupe called from the kitchen and came through the door to greet me. "Where have you been these days?"

"Well," I replied, "with the cold I have stayed in Quetzalan, but I finally had to come here to see our grandmother."

"Our grandmother is sleeping," she said. "The cold makes her bones ache."

"I am not!" called out Rubia from her pallet in the kitchen. "Tell him to come in here where it is warm, and get us some coffee."

I followed Lupe into the kitchen and sat on the pallet next to Rubia. "How have you been, grandmother?"

"Not well," she replied. "But now, tell me, why have you come? It must be something important to come over here through the cold and clouds like this."

"You are right," I told her. "There was a dream, and I was chased by a witch."

"A witch, eh? Well, I never thought they'd go after you. You were not even here when all those witches were around. Did you get a good look at that 'thing'? Was it a man, or a woman?"

"A woman," I replied.

"Was it Doña Marta down the way?"

"No."

"Then maybe it was old María Sanchez." She ran a general store in the lower part of the village. A dark, heavy woman, she did not wear her long braids tied on the top of her head like most of the women in the village. Many said she was a witch. Her mother had been a witch.

"It wasn't her either; as a matter of fact, it wasn't anyone from around here."

"Well, you have your own witch. You'd better really be careful of that one."

I thought of the hornet's nest of academia that I had dreamed about—was this where my own personal witch came from?

"The witch that was after me slipped up somewhere," Rubia said. "Let go of my soul, she did, or I wouldn't be here now. But that doesn't mean she's gone. She's probably still down there planning some kind of evil, if she can catch me again."

I wondered about the dark places in people's psyches where witches worked. Would my witch slip up too?

"Now tell me everything that happened," she demanded.

I began my long account of the dream, and Rubia listened intently, hardly commenting until I had finished my story. I omitted rather awkwardly the tremendous help that "Cruz" had been.

"Well, she almost got you, she did," Rubia said. "You know, when you are curing, that's when you usually see those 'things'— witches, that is. Maybe they have made a deal with those Lords down there, or maybe, worse, they have done something evil themselves, something savage to the one you're trying to cure, your precious one, your little dove. If they have done something savage, then it's too late. If they haven't, if you tell those people—the precious one's family, that is—'Yes, there is a witch out there after you,' don't tell the people who that witch is. Otherwise they will hire another witch, who will do something even more horrible." She paused. "I have seen that kind of thing," she added.

"So you have to talk to people. You have to see. You have to know who likes your precious one and who wishes something bad to befall him or her. You search the dreams, but sometimes that isn't enough, you have to ask the parents and the relatives who could be doing witchcraft, and they'll probably tell you. Then, if you see the witch in dreams, you know you've got him, but those witches are hard to find. They may be dogs, or *tlacuaches,* or birds there in the darkness, and then you have to fight with them to see who they really are, to see their naked *tonal,* to see beyond the animal, the *nagual* that hides them. That's when it's really dangerous because these others, others who know the way of the ancestors, might go after you in Talocan and even here. They'll get you. They'll witch you good. There were a lot of people killed around here when witches started doing those kinds of things to one another." She propped herself up a bit better and stared off into the distance.

"When was that?" I knew that her uncle had been deeply involved in the War of Witches, and probably her mother, too. I was beginning to think that even Rubia had been part of it, though I was sure she would deny any wrongdoing.

"Well, that was a long time ago. They were all killing each other off. Maybe that was when your friend 'Cruz' got it. He just might be one of them who's still seeking justice after all these years."

"Who was he?"

"Don't know," Rubia replied, quite obviously becoming uneasy.

"Who was he?" I insisted, again.

"Well, might have been one of the Cruzes from down there," she said, motioning toward the lower half of the village. "Lots of them got it then. Their savage ways killed a lot of people, but at least now there are no more witches here in San Martín." She said this with deliberate finality.

"Why not?" I kept asking. "What happened to them all?"

"They're gone. There are no more witches!" she insisted.

I knew it was time to talk of other things. She would tell me no more.

Chapter 7

FOLLOWING THE PATH

Nine months later. September 17, 1977,
Quetzalan, Puebla, Mexico

I CAME UP TO THE SIERRA
FOR THE FESTIVAL OF SAN MIGUEL
IN ANOTHER VILLAGE
and was going to stay until
the great festival of San Francisco
in Quetzalan on the fourth of October.

My plan to photograph the festivals would leave me little time to visit San Martín. I had already obtained permission from the curates of both Quetzalan and San Miguel Tizapan to place my cameras in the bell towers and choir lofts of their churches. Photographing these festivals was no simple task. I approached it like a general marshaling his forces: positioning my equipment, checking distances, light levels, and angles.

It was hard, hot work. The rainy season had ended early, and the scorching sun was relentless. Under the eaves and in the choir lofts of the two churches, the heat was overpowering. Even the great old room I had at the hotel in Quetzalan offered little relief, as it had not rained in well over a week, and the adobe walls radiated the warmth of the day all night long.

After six or seven days, I began to have the same recurrent dream. Again and again I found myself being trapped in a hot, dark cavern. It was a short dream with little connection to anything else that I saw in the night, but finally I knew that this was building into another journey in the world of darkness. Each day the dream became slightly more elaborate. In Rubia and Inocente's terms, I was clearly heading to the southern edge of Talocan, the source of heat. In my own terms, I began to think this was occurring as part of my training. Rubia's constant reinterpretations of my dreams were having an effect: not only was I dreaming directly in the underworld, but I found I could control these travels, and I had seen no more witches. After a few days, this dream of being in the cave dominated my entire night, and I had found my dear friend "Cruz" again to guide me through that mysterious world.

IT BEGAN, I wrote in my dream journal, when my *tonal* finally left my body and entered into the hot reaches of a great cavern at the southern edge of Talocan. There was steam, smoke, and fire everywhere. There were little men, servants of the underworld, in native dress toting huge loads of firewood and tossing them onto raging fires that glowed everywhere through the darkness and smoke. Each group had its own bonfire, and the men's movements seemed synchronized, as if they were part of a dance. Alternately, they tossed in their loads and then stood back and watched the fires throwing sparks everywhere. I watched for a while and moved on.

Finding a passage behind me, I followed it, and suddenly there appeared two brilliant spirals whirling in opposite directions in a glowing, colored sky. I knew what this was; it was a recurrent hallucination from my days in the Haight-Ashbury, when everyone was integrating acid into their lives. Large doses of LSD had originally made this hallucination particularly vivid, and since then it had become good visual entertainment and a recurrent dream. Somehow I never tired of it.

The sky changed color, and a horizon line appeared. Emanating from the horizon and flowing to my feet was a checkerboard pattern of light and dark colors. From the exact center between the two swirling spiral suns, a road zigzagged out to me. Then, back on the horizon, a bright orange-yellow light began to shine and move toward me. I knew what it was, though other times it had been bright chartreuse or aquamarine.

Suddenly I felt a hand reach up and touch my shoulder. I turned and saw it was "Cruz," his deep brown eyes looking huge and shaken.

"Aren't you frightened?" he asked.

"No. This is something I've seen many times before. Don't worry, it won't get you," I told him, putting my arm on his shoulder and holding him tightly. He was obviously startled by my vision.

As the orange-yellow light came closer, it became a huge snake with long, sharp viper's fangs and glowing, red serpent's eyes. Every scale was clear and detailed. Its flaming, forked tongue shot out constantly from the hollow base of its mouth. Once, perhaps, this had been a terrifying sight, but having seen it so many times, I rather enjoyed the visual effects, knowing that the serpent never reached me. Snakes never frightened me, and I liked this one. Cruz was holding on tighter and tighter.

I looked at him and said, "Don't worry, younger brother, this is only the color of fire that you see. It will not consume you." And the snake didn't. It came to within a few feet of us as it usually did, waving its huge head, which was half as big as I was, and opening its hissing mouth. For me, it was like seeing one of the dioramas in an old fun-house ride. I watched it for a bit and then turned. Cruz was still holding on tight. He was terrified.

"It'll eat us!" he exclaimed.

"No it won't," I told him. "If it did, it would just mean more fun and color. This is one of the things that I know."

"Looks to me like it might be the Colohuetzin," Cruz blurted out.

"It's not," I assured him. I had heard many descriptions of the earth monster from Rubia and Inocente, and my little pet hallucination was definitely not it, but then I had never seen the great Lord of the fires of the South of the underworld.

"You know how to find the Colohuetzin?" I asked Cruz.

"Well, maybe," he replied.

"I know it is here someplace in Atotonican," I told him.

"They say that he lives near the bubbling springs," Cruz said.

"How do we get there? Let's go."

"Oh, you don't want to see him. He is dangerous and causes much suffering. Why, we'd probably burn up if we ever saw him," Cruz told me. "The Colohuetzin is the one who eats the earth, the worm with the mouth of fire that makes these caverns. We'd suffer and burn if we ever found him," the little man went on.

"No, we wouldn't. I'd just like to see him. He is the Lord of the South," I insisted.

"Well, we could fly over the springs and see if we could see that 'thing' there."

"Let's go," I replied.

"OK," he finally agreed. "There are some doves over there that we could take to see if he is at the steaming spring."

We went with the doves, climbing onto them and flying through the smoke and steam in the South of Talocan.

"What do you want to see this place for?" Cruz asked. "This is a place for suffering in the fires. This is the inferno. This is where the evil ones go to, the murderers and the witches who are caught."

As we flew through the smoke and vapor, we could see hundreds of fires below us, all stoked by the *popocamej*, the "smoke ones," and their assistants. Finally we came to a great bubbling pool in the darkness and landed on a charred black tree. There were two buzzards waiting for us.

"So you've come to see the Lord of the fires of the earth," one of them croaked. "He's down there all right, but he'll quickly turn you into cinders if he sees you. That's how we lost our head feathers. If you're very careful and wait, you'll see him in that cavern over there."

"Shame you aren't ready to become our meal yet," the other one said.

"I'm hungry," the first one remarked, and they both flew off to search for the bodies of the dead or dying. Cruz and I sat down to watch the huge bubbling spring. We talked of many things. Cruz was becoming a close friend in the world of dreams, but I still didn't understand who this strange man was or what he wanted.

As we sat watching the spring, two groups of men came. "Those are *popocamej*," Cruz informed me. "They are going to see the Lord there in the cave, and maybe we can get a look at him.

That's what you want, isn't it? If we crawl down there with the little mice, they will not notice us, and then we might see him."

"All right," I said, changing into a mouse. I was getting remarkably adept at shape shifting, and the change came quickly.

We went with the other mice behind the *popocamej*, scurrying as fast as we could deep into the cave. The *popocamej* began to speak, but I could not understand them. The chattering grew louder.

"Stop!" Cruz said. "'They' know that you are here. One of them says he smells fresh meat. We must leave here quickly, but I don't know the way out."

"But I do," I replied.

I had been to the actual cave that the local Sanmartinos regard as the southern entry to Talocan to leave offerings. Rubia had sent me there as a part of my apprenticeship. This cave was south of San Martín, near Citlaltepetl, the Pico de Orizaba, "Peak of the Stars." It was high in the rain forest in a region almost always hidden by the clouds that constantly shroud this mountain. A huge, hot river flowed from the cave and formed pools, then tumbled down the mountainside. As the water cooled, the pools formed natural baths that were both delightful and refreshing. If we followed the stream flowing from the bubbling pool we would find our way out of the underworld, I assured Cruz.

"That's too far away," he replied. "They'll surely get us before we could find that place. Let's go this way," he said, taking off down another passage in the darkness.

I followed him, but it was becoming much hotter. Fires were everywhere, but the walls seemed to be closing in on us as we ran. Suddenly, a great, dark head reared up before us. Like a worm, it had no eyes, and the body seemed to extend back into the cavern. What we could see was writhing and twisting itself up into knots and then uncoiling around the hot boulders on the floor. We quickly hid, but the monster sensed our presence, opening its mouth to reveal a blast of flame. The heat was scorching, and I could feel it all over me. It was not at all like my pet snake, and I had never seen a hallucination like this before. It was truly terrifying. We turned and started to scurry out as fast as we could.

"That was it, that was the Lord of this place," Cruz said breathlessly. I was panting. "That was the Colohuetzin, the great worm that makes the caverns and grottoes of this world and of your world, too."

We ran and ran until we were finally out of the cave. The great fires were again all around us, but now the *popocamej* had seen us, even though we were so small. We kept running and heard a great commotion behind us. "That's them! That's them!" we heard a chorus of high-pitched voices shouting. Echoes resounded all around us.

"They know we are here!" Cruz shouted. "They don't get many fleshed ones down here! They're starving; they'll strip your flesh and burn your bones!" Finally we reached the spring of boiling waters and in the great tree now were two small, black-and-white night birds. We quickly changed and took off with the two birds, but there were sparks and flames all around us.

"They're after us, and my feathers are burning," Cruz shouted. Mine were too in the conflagration that followed us. We were falling, and the fires were hotter and hotter.

"There is a stream!" Cruz called out. "Let's head there!"

Half flying and half falling through the maelstrom of flame, we managed to land right in the stream.

Ploosh! Hisss! The water puffed and steamed . . . we were safe from the flames and the *popocamej*.

There were fish in the stream, all talking with one another, opening and closing their mouths.

"They say they're swimming to the Lord and Lady of the Eastern Sea," said Cruz. "That is a land of plenty, a land of abundance, where there is no danger. Let's follow them."

We changed into fish and followed our brothers and sisters through the rushing waters, jumping and swimming over and under one another with the sound of the water around us. It was like a torrential rain at times. It was cool and wonderful to be frolicking in the waters. Up, down, over, and under, we went flowing and tumbling through the stream, over great waterfalls, ever onward toward the sea.

As the waters became more calm, we flowed over vast plains and deep green pastures beneath the waters. There were high hills and even mountains in this world of water. We entered the Great Sea of the East from the stream that took us away from the fires of the South.

Swimming through the waters, we could see other vast, rich lands below us. There were gardens and orchards with tropical fruits, mangoes, papayas, pineapples, and bananas. The fields were filled with tall cornstalks, and there were cobblestoned paths leading everywhere. There were humble but well-kept homes among the fields, and little villages dotted the landscape. It was as rich a land as I had been told.

This was the Water World that the ancient ancestors had seen as paradise. No one here had to work. The lands beneath the waters simply gave forth their bounty. When they heard about this place, the friars in the sixteenth century were astounded that a paradise could exist in what they thought of as Hell.

We saw people sitting in front of their houses and trading in the markets of the villages of the Water World. They all wore clean, white clothing like good Sanmartinos. Swimming above the paths under the sea, we could see the villages were becoming more numerous and larger.

"Let's stop here," Cruz finally said near a small, white stone house. "Here we can ask how to get to the palace."

"What palace?" I asked.

"Why, the great palace, the town hall where the Lords of this realm live. The Lord and the Lady of the Waters rule this place. The *alpixque,* the *ahuane,* and all the other 'water ones' are their servants, but their Lady, the Llorona, is almost never here. She is in the House of Women in the West. There she hunts for men unfaithful to their wives and those who do not live a good life. The Lord of the waters, though, is different. The 'water ones' bring him the *tonals* of those who have fallen in the waters or have drowned, and he holds big feasts for them and gives them anything they want. All those *tonals* who come here want to stay. This is a life without care or work. There is always plenty here. They know me here, and this is where I would want to stay, but . . . ." A look of sadness and disappointment came over my companion's face. "It is not possible yet."

We had changed into ourselves and had sat down on a bench in front of a house. A diminutive woman brought us mangoes to eat. I asked my friend repeatedly if there was something that I could do for him in the world of the living.

"You must follow the path and do no harm or evil to anyone, be of service to the Lords and to those who live on the earth. You must live a good life. I must await justice."

With this, Cruz got up and disappeared into the house. I began to awaken to the sunshine outside my window in Quetzalan. That was the last I saw of Cruz for a long, long time. Why my friend and companion had disappeared from my dreams I did not know, but I was more determined than ever to find out about him. Perhaps there was something I could do that would speed his soul to its rightful place in the waters of the underworld.

I CLOSED MY journal, resolving to go see Rubia that morning. I just might be able to cajole from her a bit more information about

"Cruz." There was something that the sorceress was not telling me about him, and at the same time old Inocente seemed overinterested in my dreamtime companion. It was confusing, to say the least.

I went downstairs in the hotel for breakfast. It was not as hot, and clouds were forming in the east toward the coast. I could feel the change in the weather coming that had been foreshadowed in my dream.

I did not have a car this time, so I asked a friend who was staying in the hotel if he could give me a ride over to the village, though I knew it would have to be after lunch. He was the local director of the National Coffee Institute, and because he never missed lunch with Doña Iris in the hotel restaurant and never went back to work in the afternoon, it would be easy. Doña Iris was by far the best cook in Quetzalan, and her midday meals were something to be savored. The fact that Fernando weighed over a hundred kilos was largely due to her culinary efforts. Though he had lived in Quetzalan for over two years, he still stayed at the hotel, I think to be closer to her food.

It was midafternoon and already raining when I was dropped off at the church of San Martín and made my way up to Doña Rubia's house. The door was locked, and she was not at home.

I went back down to the church hoping to find another ride back to Quetzalan and heard Padre Guillermo there, softly playing his guitar and singing. Guillermo was a Spanish Franciscan, whose order, after much convincing, had released him from his monastery near Tepoztlan in the Valley of Morelos to become a parish priest in this little town. A member of the Catholic Action group, dedicated to helping develop the rural economy, Guillermo was a very progressive prelate who integrated social development, liberation theology, and a deep concern for the villagers into his religious practice.

I had given Guillermo his first lessons in Nahuat, but after two years in the village he spoke the language as well as I did, or better.

He preached and prayed in the local dialect of Modern Aztec and even said part of the mass in it. This was not really authorized, as there was no official church translation into Nahuat.

Guillermo brought out a bottle of good Spanish red wine, and we sat and talked, listening for a vehicle returning to Quetzalan in the rain. He had become a close friend and confidant of Rubia's. The old sorceress never missed his Tuesday evening study groups and was helping to translate, not only the Gospels, but parts of the mass and the Epistles into Nahuat, too. Guillermo's ministry was quite a contrast to that of the friars of the sixteenth century, who saw anything native as idolatrous or sacrilegious. He openly tried to incorporate native traditions and beliefs into Catholic liturgy and theology.

Under Guillermo the preparations for the local saint's day had become more lavish and spectacular, while being made less expensive for the *mayordomo* in charge. He organized local dance groups to perform in other villages and in state and national competitions, which defrayed much of the cost of their colorful costumes. He was also instrumental in helping me obtain permission to use the lofts and bell towers of local churches to set up my cameras.

The afternoon wore on, and we talked about the marriages, baptisms, and funerals at which he had officiated. He confided in me that he had had so much *mole,* the rich chocolate chili sauce that was a staple at any elegant meal in town, that he was beginning to hate the stuff. We continued to talk, and he played his guitar. He was working on a new hymn for mass that he had translated into Nahuat. His translation was as good as anything I had ever heard. We talked about Rubia and her seemingly double life—an Aztec *curandera* and a Catholic Action activist. In a way, their concerns were the same—the welfare of Sanmartinos—but one served the earth, and the other the sky. This was one of the first hints I had had about the true nature of worship in the Sierra. This was not "syncretism" the way the textbooks wrote about it. It was something very different. A person up here in the Sierra was in one belief system or in the other; they did not overlap or conflict. Yet, perhaps because all these systems had been made by human beings, there were essential similarities. We drank on and watched the rain fall.

Finally, after several hours without any sign of a vehicle, I decided to see if Doña Rubia had returned home yet. I climbed the hill, and when I got to Rubia's house the door was open and she was home.

"The night is coming, good afternoon," I said in greeting and stepped into the house. Lupe came into the main room and told me Rubia was now resting. She had spent most of the previous night assisting with the birth of a baby boy at the Santos house up the hill. I said that I would wait; Lupe brought me a large cup of coffee, and I sat down on a low stool. As I slowly sipped my coffee, I reflected on my dream and the situation of my strange friend "Cruz," as well as my afternoon with Padre Guillermo. Rubia slept for at least another hour, and by that time I was rather anxious to get back to Quetzalan. It was beginning to get dark.

She hobbled into the room with her prim white shift over her blouse, her ever-present black necklace, and a smile on her face. She was obviously refreshed by her nap.

"I heard you helped a new boy into the light," I said.

"Sure did, but this one really wanted to come out. He was good and ripe, well cooked."

"There were no problems?"

"None at all," she replied. "Doña Rosa has had five now, and they just pop right out of her. What are you doing here anyway? I didn't think you would be by."

"Well," I said, "I had another dream, a good one." I began to recount the tale of my dream, judiciously holding back much of the material about "Cruz."

When I had finished, she said, "So you were in the Great Sea. That's a tough place to get a soul out of. It's so good there that they all want to stay. Might be a good idea to leave something, maybe by a stream or at the well, for the Lords of that place. Even though you didn't see 'them,' they can be very helpful sometimes. It's a good idea to leave offerings for them. Once in a while they'll even send a soul back that wants to stay with them.

"Last time I was there, there was a girl who had fallen off the rocks while her mother was doing the wash down below, near the wide part of the river. That little one almost drowned, and they got her soul for sure. Those water ones, the *ahuane*, took her all the way to the palace of the Lords there. When the girl was finally brought to me, she was barely breathing. We kept her warm and kept a vigil for her for three whole days. I put out a lot of tobacco, and we burned candles and incense the whole time. I prayed a lot for that little one. I told them there in the water that I was coming down to look for her, and I did. I placed a large jar of water at the base of the family altar and watched it carefully for any sign of the girl, but had no luck.

"Finally I went in there. I entered through the well down there," she said, motioning toward the town well, "and I followed the stream, not with the fish the way you did, but with a little frog. I went farther and farther until I came to the giant green river and the deep part of the Great Sea. I followed the roads and kept to the royal highways down there.

"I went through villages and towns with huge buildings. You know, they even have buses down there for the great highways under the sea, and I rode the bus all the way to the capital of the place. You don't even have to pay them. You just get on. That's how rich they are down there in the Water World.

"I got off the bus in the plaza and went straight over to the *palacio*. It was huge, with big, heavy doors. The guards, the *alpixque*, let me right in, and I walked down a long hall to where they were feasting. He was there, that one, the Lord, and so were all of his *compadres:* the *presidente* and the *mayordomos* of the sea. They were all eating big, fat fish, and there were mountains of tortillas, fruits, and beans and rice, and big *cazuelas* of tasty stews.

"'Come in!' he said to me, 'Have some of our tasty food!' But I didn't want any. It's so good there that if you partake, if you eat there once, you will never want to return. You're lucky you only had some mangoes there, but I'll bet they were the best mangoes you ever ate.

"'I come for a favor, O sir, O great Lord,' I addressed the Lord of that place.

"'What is it you wish, grandmother?' he asked.

"'There is a little one, a little dove who is one of ours; she is a precious thing, and all above weep for her. She has fallen in the waters near the great wide stream, and she will not come back to us on the earth. Her mother weeps. Her father weeps. Her grandmothers and grandfathers weep. Her uncles and aunts weep; all of her brothers and sisters on the earth weep for her, O sir.

"'It is not her time to live with you here. She yet has much life along her road, and her light burns bright. She is but a child who laughs and sings. She needs the light to become ripe and bear fruit. Perhaps her mother, her aunts, were not careful, not vigilant. She has fallen into the waters, and now she will not come back to us. Please, O Lord, I beseech you, I ask you, return her to us so that she may see the Holy Light once more.

"'If she is with you, send her forth, let her come back to us on the earth. Please, O Lord, with a hundred prayers, a thousand prayers and much love, I ask you to send this little dove back to the world of the light.'

"That's what I told him there in the waters, and he sent his henchmen out to look for her. They brought her into the feast. She had a new blouse and a new dress, and her head was piled high with a *mecapal.* The little one looked like a lady.

"'Shall she stay here with us?' the Lord asked his *compadres:* his *presidente,* the commander; his *jueces,* the judges; his *aguaciles,* the executioners; and his *mayordomos,* who were in charge of his festivals. There was much commotion and much discussion.

"Finally, he turned to the girl and said, 'You may stay if you wish and join our feast.'

"'O little one,' I told her, 'your parents weep for you; your grandparents weep for you; your aunts and uncles weep for you there in the light. You have much to do yet in the light. You will become ripe and bear fruit. You will marry and have children, many of them. You will become an honored grandmother. Do not stay here in the darkness. It is not good. You will have many things when you come back to us on the earth. There will be new clothes, tasty food, toys, and your parents. Your grandparents, your aunts and uncles, your brothers and sisters will all rejoice.'

"The little one said nothing, and I bid the Lord and his minions farewell with much respect and returned here, right to the place where she fell in the water, where the women of the village wash.

"I told her mother to lay a path of flowers so that her lost soul could find its way back from the waters, and I told her father to get a chicken for a savory stew. I told her aunts and uncles to bring new clothes and gifts if they wanted her to return and to put them all in front of the jug of water at the altar so that she would see them through the waters. We kept a vigil all night, and in the morning she began to return to us here on the earth. The Lord of the waters let her poor little soul return to us here in the light!"

After Rubia's tale finished, I asked again about "Cruz," but she was just as evasive as before. I began the long walk back to Quetzalan. The rain had stopped. The moon lit my way as I passed the cemetery.

Chapter 8

CURING AND KILLING

IT WAS SHORTLY AFTER MY RETURN
TO MEXICO CITY THAT A COUPLE
FROM SAN MARTÍN
CAME TO MY DOOR.
Their nine-year-old daughter
was suffering from magical fright.
I had no idea what to do. They were seeking help for her
that was obviously beyond simple economic aid.

She was ill, and they were lost in the masses of the dispossessed living at the edges of the city. Money and a job would have done them some good, but that was not what they sought.

Where they lived was one of Mexico's "lost cities," miles of ramshackle housing erected on unoccupied land at the outskirts of the city. Millions from rural Mexico pressed into the lost cities in hope of finding work, but few did. I knew the kind of stress and difficulty that these people were living under. Several years before, I had lived for a while with a family of masons I knew in Mexico's most notorious *ciudad perdida*, Netzahualcoyotl.

Most people in Mexico were blind to these conditions. They could look at what was happening along the streets and boulevards day in and day out without ever seeing a thing. Mexico's lost cities are truly lost, vast stretches of urban poverty along major thoroughfares, sometimes even shielded from view by Potemkin village facades and inaccessible to most public transportation. Few but the masses who lived along those filthy, muddy, dusty streets would ever venture into them.

Despite their hard lot, most residents of the lost cities are bright and helpful, though they live in *la miseria,* a collective condition that describes the entire result of the crowding, poverty, and destitution. Most live in large extended families of eighteen to twenty people sharing one or two rooms, sleeping in shifts, and sharing meager meals of beans and tortillas. If one or two members of a household have a job, then all can survive, but barely.

Raul and María García were waiting for me on my doorstep with their daughter, Erlinda, when I returned from the university. Even before entering the house, we established that I was a *compadre* to the saint of a mutual friend who was the godfather of their daughter. I had given this man an image of his patron saint for his family altar and during his saint's day celebration had sponsored the erection of a cross.

My relationship with Rubia and Inocente was now widely known in the village. Rubia had been touting me as a competent curer to many people for quite a while, and with her help I had already managed two or three healings. The couple had come to ask me to cure their daughter and to search out her lost soul in Talocan.

Raul had on a tattered shirt and jeans, both repaired many, many times. María wore a traditional blouse that also showed signs of constant repair and a black polyester skirt along with ill-fitting black shoes. Their daughter wore a brightly colored print shift and had ribbons braided into her long pigtails. She was barefoot. These were obviously the Garcías' formal clothes. They had been waiting for me to come back from the university since midmorning.

Doña Marta, my maid, had insisted they wait out in front of the house on the stoop. She did not approve of inviting Indians into the house, though her own recent forebears were most probably *indigenas*. I decided to risk Marta's ire and invite the Garcías in, explaining that they were *compadres*. This was something that even Marta could understand—godparents and sponsors are considered like kin throughout Mexico.

I opened the door and led them into the dining room, with its big, battered table that I had salvaged from a ruined hacienda near Cholula. "Please, may you seat yourselves," I bid them in very formal Nahuat, as we were using the rather formal and affected speech of *compadres*.

I went into the kitchen to ask Marta to bring out some *yolixpa*, the green-herbed firewater from the Sierra de Puebla. I also wanted to see if she had enough on the stove so that I could invite the Garcías to lunch. She did, although I could imagine her indignation at having to serve Indians. I asked her to bring beans, rice, plenty of tortillas, hot sauce, and a bit of her chicken in green sauce to the coffee table with some plates and utensils for us.

When I went back into the dining room, María was looking at a cradle board from the village that I had on the wall, and Erlinda was counting the stitches on a piece of embroidery that we used as a wall hanging. Raul was fidgeting uncomfortably in a straight-backed chair. My hunch was that the Garcías had never been in a house that did not have dirt floors or that had more than two rooms. I decided that they would be more comfortable in the living room, where at least there were some low stools like the ones from their home in the Sierra.

We continued talking about friends and family in the village. María was a font of local gossip from the Sierra. Though she had lived here in Mexico City for almost five years, she knew everything that was going on in San Martín. I made a concerted effort to keep her in the conversation, as usually men go off with the men to talk about work and their fields while the women gather in the kitchen to gossip among themselves. Raul remarked about my unusual earth altar, and at first I didn't understand what he was talking about. I had an earth altar, but it was upstairs in the study. He had mistaken the fireplace and the things on the mantle for a traditional family altar. It did dominate the room like a traditional altar. The pictures of my family and brightly colored Mexican paintings above the fireplace would be appropriate for a traditional altar, but there wasn't the usual garland of saints' pictures, so he wondered if I was a Catholic. I was, I assured him, at least as Catholic as he was.

Finally Marta brought out a big tray with our lunch on it. The living room was not carpeted, and so it would be much easier for Marta to clean up. It is rather difficult to explain to people who are used to having the chickens, cats, dogs, and occasional pig nosing around on the floor to be careful and not spill anything. The floor would be a mess by the time we finished. Few utensils are used in the Sierra, with the exception of the spoon for soups. Almost everything is eaten by using tortillas to pick up the food.

Erlinda, or Linda, as everyone called her, picked at her food, eating almost nothing.

"Have some of these big fat beans and tortillas, my little dove," María admonished. But the child ate almost nothing. She just stared at the floor listlessly.

María gave a sigh and asked no one in particular, "What will I do? This little puppy eats almost nothing and is always awake. Perhaps it is her animal that they've got; she is always sick. Surely she needs her strength," implying that perhaps the child was bewitched and her *nagual* was being held somewhere in the underworld.

After much talk, Raul finally asked me in a very formal way if I could help them by finding their daughter's soul. They had explained all her symptoms, and it seemed a classic case of soul loss. I had never done a curing without Rubia's expert advice, but I could see that in this case I would have to try. The Sierra was far away.

"Let's go upstairs to where I have a real altar," I said to Raul. "I have some copal and some candles there."

Because Marta obviously wanted us out of the living room so that she could clean up and go home, I led the Garcías up to my study. My altar in the corner was nothing like the altars that dominated every household in the Sierra. For someone who didn't know what it was, it was unrecognizable as an altar. It was just a few sherds, some candles, and an incense burner on a bookshelf. I lit one of the candles and laid an old *serape* down on the floor for Linda. I told her to lie down, and standing with her parents, I began a short prayer to the earth.

When I had finished, I turned to Raul and said, "Well, let's see if it's an evil wind that got her." María knelt down and loosened the girl's clothes.

Linda was tense. I began by massaging her hands, muttering little terms of endearment softly to her in Nahuat, "My little dove, little one, precious thing, little jade." As she relaxed I began to examine her abdomen and her neck. The abdomen was bloated. I knew I wanted a doctor to see her. I turned to Raul and said, "Well, it's not an evil wind, and probably not a witch. There is no cold wind in this little one, and I feel nothing has entered her. Where could she have lost her soul?" I asked the parents.

"We don't know," replied Raul.

"Has she fallen, or hurt herself?" I asked. These were the most common ways a soul was lost.

"I don't know," Raul replied.

"Linda, my little one, my dear, have you fallen, or hit your head somewhere?" I asked the little girl.

"No, sir," she replied, "not that I remember, sir."

"Well, maybe she does not remember, but perhaps she did fall. Perhaps your brothers or sister, her aunt or uncles, may remember."

Raul and María had already explained that they lived with two of his brothers and a sister. I knew that we would have to go to their home to get to the bottom of this.

"We should go to see them, but first there is a friend, a *medico*, who I would like to have a look at Linda. He won't cost you anything, and he is a very good man."

I went to the phone and called Luis Maldonado, the husband of one of my colleagues, who had his offices a few blocks away. I caught him at home before he left for his office, and he agreed to stop over to examine the girl.

Luis was downstairs ringing the bell even before I had finished talking about Linda's sickness with her parents. They were certain it was a case of soul loss. I went down to let him in and brought him up to the study. Marta had finished already and left. The house was empty except for us.

Luis had an easy bedside manner and explained to Raul and María that he too wanted to examine Linda.

"It seems as though it may be some type of parasite," I told him in English. "Her abdomen is bloated, but there is no pain that I could find."

"You're probably right, but there are a few other things I want to check." Luis did not have the usual black bag with him, but he had a stethoscope in his pocket. He brought it out and warmed it up.

"Now, Linda, my little dove, Dr. Luis wants to listen to the winds in you. Breathe deeply," I said to her in Nahuat. As Luis examined her, I translated, though she spoke Spanish quite well. Luis checked her eyes, her throat, and her ears as best he could.

"Does she ever vomit?" Luis asked Raul in Spanish. "Or are there worms in her stools?"

"Sometimes," María replied for her husband, "but little worms, no."

"Not even the round things that twist the insides?" I asked her in Nahuat, as I suspected she hadn't quite understood in Spanish.

"Well, those things. Yes, sometimes," María said. "She says there are worms sometimes," I told Luis in English.

"If there are worms, then those are the first things we have to get rid of. There are a couple of medications I can prescribe."

"What about an epazote tea?" I asked. "That's probably the most common vermifuge in the Sierra."

"It's as good as what I could prescribe," he said in English. "She is a bit underweight and small for her age. I don't like giving some of those prescription medications to children. They're quite toxic, you know. We ought to get a stool sample, though, just to see what other things she might have."

"That might be difficult," I told him, "but we can try."

"I have specimen containers at the office," Luis said. "I would like to examine her there, but I'm already late for my first patients. It would be a while before I could see her."

"I'm going to give them a ride back to Ixtapalapa, where they live, and I could stop at your office on the way for the sample containers," I told him. "Maybe it would be better to see her another day at the office when you don't have other patients." I didn't think an office visit would be at all comfortable for either the Garcías or Luis's patients, as they were mostly middle-class Mexicans who never mixed with Indians.

Luis left, and I offered the Garcías a ride home. We stopped on the way for the sample containers. I didn't know whether the Garcías would use them.

It was a long drive through traffic to Ixtapalapa. The street was so rutted that I had to park the car almost a kilometer from their shanty, but the walk was pleasant through the dusty streets alive with people. Many people knew the Garcías and stopped to chat with us on the way.

The García home looked like all the rest: two rooms and a cook shack made up of odd sizes of corrugated tin, tar paper, and slats of old wood. Newspapers were jammed into some of the larger holes. The front yard was dusty, but there were some flowers struggling to grow.

Raul's brother, Alejandro, rose from where he was sitting on a couple of old automobile tires to greet us. He apologized that his other brother Miguel was still at work, doing construction someplace on the other side of the city. He invited us in. Ducking to get through the low door, the first thing I saw was a large family altar just like the ones in the Sierra. Linda, I noticed, stayed outside.

Alejandro got out a Western-style chair for me and put it at the table in front of the altar. "This man is a healer?" he asked his family in Nahuat. "Doesn't look like any of them I've ever seen."

"Shhh! This one speaks!" Raul said, meaning that I spoke Nahuat.

"Yes I do," I told him in Nahuat, "and I know the Most Holy Earth and the Land of Darkness too. You know the old ones, Rubia and Inocente? They were the ones who showed me the path."

Alejandro was obviously shocked and probably a bit embarrassed. "O, I am so sorry, sir. It's just that—well, most *curanderos*, healers, are, well, er, ummmm, not gringos . . . ."

"Well, what about Erlinda? Do you think it's soul loss? And where did she lose her soul?" I moved directly to the matter at hand, a technique I had learned from Rubia.

"Well, yes, look at her out there," he said pointing out the door. "She just sits there while the rest of them play."

Alejandro was right. Linda was just sitting on a rock while the rest of the children played in a makeshift house drawn in the dust.

"How many of the children are yours?" I asked.

"Oh, I have five," he replied.

"And how many other children live here?"

"Well, our sister Julia has four, and her daughter Lupe has two more. Miguel, the mason, has four too, but they're in Puebla with his wife," Alejandro explained.

Almost all the children living there were between the ages of three and eleven. Erlinda had quite an extended family to play with, and there were plenty of other children around, but she didn't seem to want to do much of anything. I could see her outside through the open door, still sitting on the rock watching the street activities. There were some other children playing not far away. Alejandro's wife, Rosa, came in from the other room with Julia, her sister-in-law.

"Hey, look! This is the *curandero*, the healer that they brought back!" Alejandro blurted out. The two women were a little shocked too.

"O, sir, I am so sorry we have nothing to offer you in our little shack," Rosa said.

"Perhaps everyone would like a beer," I said. "If you will go out and get them, I will buy them."

"Well, Don Antonio has beer."

"María, could you go over to Don Antonio's?" Rosa asked, and I gave her fifty pesos. While we waited for the beers, we chatted politely, and I managed to learn some more about Linda. She seemed to be a marginal figure in this family, perhaps because she was the only one without brothers and sisters. This didn't explain everything, however.

The beers came and, after a while, it was getting toward sunset. I knew that I didn't want to walk the rutted path to the road in the dark, so I suggested that before the holy light of the sun was gone we, or I, should pray for a dream. I told María that they would have to get some things for the altar: flowers, a dish of water, some grains of corn, and two types of candles. I gave her money for the candles.

When she returned, we called Linda in and began the prayers. Rosa put a few coals from the fire into the censer she took from below the altar, and I burned some of the copal I had brought along.

I then lit the tapers and the votive candle, mumbling,

> *Nican in talocan*
> Here in the talocan,
> *Nicanin yohualichan*
> Here in the house of darkness,
> *nimechtatauhtia nen conetzin nen espiritu.*
> I beseech you—this child—her spirit.
> *Nican nimechaxcatili ica tantos oraciones*
> Here I offer you such prayers.
> *Nican nimechtemaktia nofuerza notonal.*
> Here, I let you have all my strength, my soul.

Cani yetoc nejin?
　　Where is this one?
Cani ancpiaj toconetzin?
　　Where is our child being kept? . . .

Then I asked Linda to stand at the altar, where I blew incense over her and gave her the two tapers, telling her to walk outside with them. They were both blown out before she got to the door. I told her to come back, telling her that this was a good sign: she would be kept in the light. I then rolled the two wax candles over her arms and throat and told her she should go to bed early after drinking her epazote tea.

I told María how to prepare the tea and that I would need the stool sample for Luis. I would try to find the little girl's soul that night in my dreams. They should come to see me in a day or two. Raul and Alejandro accompanied me to the car. There was a lot more I had to find out about the Garcías before I could really cure their daughter.

IT WAS QUITE late by the time I made it back home through the rush hour traffic. The telephone office in Quetzalan was already closed. I couldn't even have a message sent to the village to have Rubia call me.

I telephoned Luis and found him still in his office. He was pretty sure the girl had parasites and also said that she was probably malnourished. She also showed some signs of a vitamin deficiency, but none of that explained the symptoms that her parents had described. It sounded to him much more like some type of social malaise.

"It is," I agreed, and told him what I had seen at the Garcías'. What I had observed, coupled with the fact that the girl wasn't eating or sleeping, made her condition rather serious. I had seen people die of this type of soul loss, I told Luis. It was a progressive condition that fed off itself, as well as off people's fears about it. Luis agreed that the girl's medical problems were probably not any more serious than those of most children living under the same conditions, but said that he would make sure there was nothing else that he could treat. He wished me luck in resolving her other problems, and I thanked him.

I went upstairs to my study, lit the candles, did some reading, and said a few short prayers while I thought about the little girl.

Suddenly I saw the great, gaping cave mouth and felt myself being blown into it, down a deep, whirling spiral, spinning and turning. Then I was in a coffee garden with well-manicured plots around each bush. There were people in native dress picking coffee and talking, but I could not understand the gossip. As I wandered through the plantation, there were fewer and fewer people, and I could hear rushing water. There was a swift stream in front of me, and I crossed it, jumping over the stepping stones. On the other side of the stream was a female *tlacuache* dressed in a native skirt with a large *mecapal* on her head.

"Where are you walking to? What path do you take?" I asked her.

She answered with a screechy voice, "Up the hill, up the hill!" So I followed along, feeling my beard and body hair growing into a gray fur coat. Slowly my nails began to grow out of the ends of my fingers, and I was becoming a possum. I dropped down to all fours, and we went along the ground. Then we were leaping through the trees, traveling faster and faster.

There were houses and a street, not unlike the street I lived on in Mexico City. The *tlacuache* I was with had disappeared. I shuffled down the street, sniffing the air. There were women out sweeping, our German neighbor Helga, Mrs. Martinez from down the street, and our local gossip Mrs. Aceves. None of them called out or spoke to me, but I said good morning to them all. It was as if I were not there. They saw me as a *tlacuache*.

When I got to the end of the street, I entered a long, columned patio, something like the courtyard in the monastery of Santo Domingo in Oaxaca. It was full of nuns dressed like penguins. They were wearing the old Notre Dame habits with starched, white wimples and black veils. I thought I recognized some of them as teachers I had had as a child.

Finally, one particularly stern-looking old nun called out to me, "Come here!" I felt like a small child facing authority again. I was sure I was in trouble with the old nun. Her face was constantly changing. I could see my aunts who had been nuns and several of my teachers, the mother superior of the convent I had worked in, and Sister Dominica, whom my father always had an eye for.

"Now follow me!" barked the big nun. I walked behind her, trying to do the penguin step she did, back and forth. As boys working at the Notre Dame convent we always joked about the way the nuns walked and spent hours imitating every variation of the curious penguin step. Even as a solemn crossbearer in front of a procession of two hundred nuns, I could make my fellow acolytes break into laughter by doing its many variations.

The big nun disappeared into the darkness. It was hot, with billowing white clouds of steam, and there was a table set with mounds of fruit, rice, and tortillas. In the center there were two huge lobsters dancing, or perhaps dueling with their huge claws, as I watched. One was a female with long black hair. The claws turned to sabers, and the lobsters were fencing on a bright, barren desert plain. I had become like them; I was one of the lobsters parrying and lunging until I fell with exhaustion.

I rolled over into a steamy world again and could feel myself being massaged all over by a thousand hands. It was very bright, and I began to awaken. It was morning in my study.

After Marta had brought up coffee, I went downstairs and called Quetzalan, leaving a message for Rubia that I would call her in the afternoon. I went to the university still thinking about Erlinda. I talked about her situation with a couple of my colleagues, but no one had any suggestions except that it would probably help if I could find Raul a job. I made a few phone calls but found nothing immediately.

When I got home that afternoon, the first thing I did was call Rubia at the appointed hour. She listened to my dream and thought it was quite auspicious.

"Well, that was the House of Women. You ought to know that. The House of Women is where the souls of women go in Talocan. It is where they can live and do no work. There is no cooking there and no weaving. They don't have to sweep or carry water. They all want to stay there forever.

"They all seek the House of Women there in Talocan. The women never leave it. The Acihuat and the Ejecacihuat are there. They all help care for the women, and they capture the men who are unfaithful for their food. That is what all those women eat," she said, with a rather sinister glee.

"There must be some powerful witches there," I remarked.

"No," said Rubia, "there are no witches there. They will not have any witches there. Witches do foul and evil things to one another. All the women of the West live together with the grandmothers and midwives, the women who have died in giving birth and the women who have fallen or drowned on the earth. They have to live there together in peace. There are no witches. The women there live almost as well as those saints in the holy light, and they help Our Lord, the sun, when he is exhausted after the day.

"If the little one is there in the House of Women, she is being well cared for. She may never want to leave there, and you won't get her soul back. I'm going to talk to her grandmothers here and see what they say about the Garcías. María, you know, is a Sanchez. Her uncle, in our terms, was the brother of Don Pedro's father. Don Pedro should be the one to help cure this little dove."

"Why didn't they go to Don Pedro, then?" I asked Rubia.

"Well, you are there in the city, and he is not, but maybe Don Pedro will help. You tell the Garcías your dream, and I will talk to the little one's grandmothers. You tell this telephone place I will be here tomorrow at the same time.

"When you tell them that dream, make sure that you open your eyes and see where the girl could have fallen. Maybe it is her cousins, uncles, or aunts who know, but just aren't saying. Maybe they don't know that they have seen this little one's soul leave her. You ask them. Make them talk about it. You are the one who has to find out what happened to the little one's soul and why you dream of the House of Women." There was a great deal of static on the line, but I could still hear Rubia without much difficulty. Her voice was strong.

"I don't think there was a witch there," she continued, "or you wouldn't have entered Talocan through the Eastern Earth Mouth. There are places that witches enter, like the Bat Water Cave and the Smoke Cave. Those are places that witches go to, and if there was a witch you would have seen one of those places. Those were the places all the witches went when they were doing their evil deeds here in San Martín."

"When was that, Doña Rubia?" I was still hoping to get more information about the War of Witches.

"That was a long time ago when the witches were all killing off one another. María's uncle was one of them, and he got it, so did her grandfather, but they were witches, anyway."

"Who were the witches?"

"Well, they were all witches. Don't concern yourself with them, or they could get you too. I told you there was no witch involved in this matter. So, we can talk tomorrow, and I will see what I can do to help this poor little one. Her soul is in your care now." And with that, Rubia hung up. She still hadn't learned much about the pleasantries of telephone etiquette, like saying good-bye.

The next morning I went back to see the Garcías and told them my dream. It didn't seem to resolve much, but we spent several hours discussing it. I began to see what was going on in the García household. This time it was raining, and many of the children were in the house, scurrying about underfoot. Miguel, the mason, Raul's brother, was the only one with a regular job, so he was gone. Their sister, Julia, obviously ran the household, along with Alejandro's wife. It was only their children who helped in the kitchen and with all the household chores. María and Raul, latecomers to this busy household, had little to do and, in fact, were looking for other housing. They had been looking for almost a year now. Erlinda was shooed out of the kitchen whenever she went in, and her mother had no real place in it either. Raul was usually gone during the day, looking for work as a laborer.

I wound my way back home through the muddy streets, the burros, and the traffic thinking about this situation. It wasn't until late afternoon that I called Rubia.

She was waiting for me. She began by telling me all the local gossip about the Garcías. José, the eldest brother, still lived in the village and had forced his brothers and sister to leave when their father died. Raul's mother and María's mother were not only friends but cousins, a relationship a bit too close for marriage, Rubia remarked. José didn't make enough on coffee to keep the family very well, but his mother, who was still alive and living with them, had never forgiven him for pushing out first Alejandro, then Miguel, and finally Raul and his wife. It was probably not actually José who forced them to leave but economic necessity; nevertheless, it was a source of continuing disharmony.

Rubia had also arranged for Don Pedro Sanchez, who owned the general store near Rubia's house, to help cure the little girl. He was, after all, an uncle of sorts. He would have the curing at his house in two weeks, and I was told to bring the Garcías up to the Sierra at that time. Meanwhile, she told me to keep on seeking a dream that would help. I knew that the Garcías needed more help than dreams could give them, and I thought I would try to get Raul a job as an assistant janitor at the university. Also Marta, our maid, agreed to take María along when she cleaned our colleague's houses and help her learn how to take care of a house. Erlinda was to accompany them, along with Marta's daughter, Aurora. It would be free help for Marta, and I gave María enough for transportation. Erlinda and Aurora, I hoped, would become friends.

The next time I visited the Garcías, Aurora and Marta were visiting. The two little girls played together almost the whole time I was there. Little Linda was better—Luis was treating her for dysentery, which had shown up in the samples, as well as a vitamin deficiency—but still not completely well. She still seemed to be marginalized in her own home. Her playing with Aurora, but not with her cousins or any of the other neighborhood children, was quite unusual.

IT WAS LATE on a Friday night when we finally came around the last tortuous curves on the rutted road to San Martín. Linda was fast asleep. Even the bouncing and jostling of those last few kilometers of dirt trail hadn't awakened her. I dropped Raul, María, and Linda off at José's. Raul's mother was delighted to see her granddaughter and immediately helped the still sleepy little girl into the house. Raul and José were quite formal, but cordial. María seemed out of place. I told them I would see them in the morning and drove back to Quetzalan through the cold fog.

The next morning I returned to San Martín and went for coffee with Rubia, who caught me up on all the town gossip. Then I went up to see Don Pedro Sanchez, María's uncle.

He was waiting on a customer in his store but immediately turned to me and said, "Well, you're here. We have work to do to find that little one's soul. You'll have to bring some things," and he started in on a long list of offerings. For Don Pedro this was strictly business. I had to pay him, even though he was quite well off by village standards, and he assumed I was passing the cost along to the Garcías.

"I'll get what we need and be back shortly," I told him. He turned and went back to his customer.

I had little trouble getting the offerings and soon returned to Pedro's barren little general store. Pedro lifted the top on the counter and brought me into the house. He sold great quantities of *aguardiente,* and his store was more like a bar at times than a general store, with a regular crowd of drunks hanging out in front. There was little on the shelves, but there were always barrels of *refino.* Actually, he made most of his money buying and selling coffee. Pedro's wife went out in front, and Pedro asked me about my dreams, though he had already heard about them from Rubia and agreed with her prognosis. We then began to arrange things on his altar.

There were dozens of old photos of his ancestors, some in antique dark wooden frames and some simply propped up against implements of the altar or tacked onto the wall. As we worked, he began to explain who was pictured in each of the yellowed photos.

"This was my father, and this one is another of my father when they finished the school," he said, pointing to a turn-of-the-century group photo of somber Indians. For some reason villagers always preferred to look very serious when having their photos taken.

"That one is Martín Cruz, and there is José Santos, and there is Miguel Cruz, and the little one is old Antonio Cruz. He lives down the way, below the well."

At this point I couldn't resist asking him about the Cruz family and, in particular, if there was someone like my "friend" in the world of dreams. Had I perhaps seen a picture somewhere else that resembled him? None of the Cruzes in the group photo on Pedro's altar had a mustache. In fact, facial hair on Indians is usually quite sparse.

"Was there one of them with long black hair and a little *bigote*, a mustache?" I asked.

"Well, let me see. None of them that I knew well had a mustache, but there was one—he was a friend of my father—his name was Arcadio Cruz. I saw him often. He was a very good man, but you know, the witches got him. They got him when I was just a boy. Maybe I have a picture of him here," he said, reaching into the trunk below his altar for an old scrapbook. Paging through the book, he pointed out all his relatives and friends.

"What about the witches?" I asked. "Were there really a lot of them?"

"There sure were." Pointing to an old photo of six men and a horse, he continued, "This one is Rubia's uncle. He was one of the worst witches. Snuffed out a lot of candles, that one did. Rubia's mother, his sister, was one of them too, and they got her. The one there is old Inocente," he said, pointing to a very young, slight man with jet black hair holding the horse. "He learned how to get them from Don Raul, Rubia's uncle. He was a *pistolero* for old Don Antonio in Ahueta, but he learned the way to do it without a gun. They couldn't hang him if he didn't use a gun. If he had not learned 'the path' from Raul, he would have been stretched from some tree long ago."

"Oh, yes?"

"Sure, that old man has killed more with his prayers than he ever did with a gun. He and Raul, Rubia's uncle, were 'brothers,' and my father, too. The other one there in the picture is my uncle José. The witches got him too.

"Now this picture should have Arcadio Cruz," he said, pointing to another yellowing group photo with dancers in front of the church of Quetzalan. The church was only partly finished at the time—the photo must have dated to the 1920s or '30s.

"Yes, right there." He pointed at a very distinguished little man in the front row with a small mustache. "There is Arcadio Cruz."

The old yellow photo was small and fuzzy, but he looked like the little man I had seen in my dreams! "He was a witch, too?" I asked, rather excited.

"Sure was," Pedro replied. "Most of them were witches. You know, with each of the animals there is something good and something foul that you can do. Every one of those animals is a killer, and witches sure use them to kill. They ask the Lords of the Most Holy Earth to give them justice, then they make sure that there is justice. Yes, that is what they do! That is the way a witch works. They are not the ones who really kill, they just help the Lords find justice for their victims.

"When there were all those witches, they were all using their animals to kill," he said in Nahuat, making a pun with the word for witch, *nagualli,* and the possessed form of someone's animal soul, *inagual.*

Pedro went on with a short account of who had killed whom in the War of Witches. He discussed who was a witch and who wasn't. I didn't ask him about Arcadio Cruz. His story of the witches didn't fit at all with what I had heard from Doña Rubia or Don Inocente.

There was a lot more to this than I had imagined. If Don Pedro was right, then half the town must have been involved with witchcraft at that time. According to his account there were far more than the dozen or so people I had heard were killed by the warring factions of witches. The actual conflict, he said, lasted almost twenty years.

As he was telling me this, an old, brittle, yellowed clipping fell out of the scrapbook and floated down to the dirt floor. The headline on it read "Modern Day Crucifixion: Indians in San Martín Crucify One of Their Own." I picked it up. There was no date on it.

"Mexican Army sent to arrest the Indians responsible for crucifixion of a native of San Martín Zinacapan," the short article began, in Spanish. Seven members of the village had been detained by the army and taken to Zacatlan. They were then handed over to the authorities in Puebla, the article continued in a tone typical of Mexican scandal sheets, enumerating all the sordid details of the event. I was looking for names and dates. Finally, at the end of the article I found the name of the victim. It was someone I had never heard of, but among those arrested were Pedro's father, the mayor of the town, the *mayordomo,* and several of his assistants.

"What is this?" I asked Pedro. "When did they crucify a witch?" I had never heard anyone in the village speak of this in all the years I had been coming here. I wondered why. Was there a conspiracy of silence about this? An event like this should have been a momentous part of village history, with the army barging in and arresting some of the most important people in the town, yet no one had ever talked about it. This didn't make sense in a place where gossip about one's neighbors and everything that had happened to them for the last twenty years is a standard form of entertainment.

"Oh, that was a lonnnggg time ago when they took my father off. He was not the killer, but they said that he was. It was a friend of his that got hung up to dry in front of the church. It was the

Cruzes and the Sandovals that got him, I think. They tied him up, nailed him up, and stuck him up in front of the church. Nobody dared go near him until he was finished. Finally, I think someone smashed the man's head in with a stone. He was out there in the plaza for a day or so, screaming at everyone that he was going to send them all to Talocan. 'You are all as good as dead,' he kept on screaming. I stayed inside, but I heard it. It was really terrifying, a real 'soul destroyer' to have to listen to all day until he kicked. It was really bad!

"That was how the War of Witches ended. The one they got was a witch all right, a real killer, a murderer. Then the army came, and they took everyone off to prison. Most people left town and went out to their coffee plantations to avoid the army. They stole everything we had left in the village. There wasn't a chicken or a pig left in town. I think that they even ate the dogs.

"My mother had to go down to Puebla to take food to my father. We all went to Puebla with her and waited for him. He was in the calaboose for a long time. I almost didn't recognize him when he got out."

Now I was really onto something.

Chapter 9

THE WAR OF WITCHES: THE BEGINNING

"HOW DID ALL THIS KILLING
GET STARTED?"
I ASKED DON PEDRO,
TRYING TO MASK MY EAGERNESS.

I sat down in a rickety old wooden chair
in front of his altar.

Don Pedro pulled up a low bench.

It seemed he wanted to talk about those times.

"Well, I don't know myself, but I can tell you what I heard when I was a boy. Those 'things' were going about killing everyone," he said. As is usual with Indians, he referred to witches in the impersonal form rather than as real people. "That friend of my father's, your man with the *bigote,* Don Arcadio Cruz, was the one who told me how it all started, at least he said he knew how it all started. He said it didn't even begin here in San Martín but at Finca El Rosal, the old coffee plantation near Quetzalan, before I was born. Don Antonio Mendez Acero was the *patrón* there.

"He fought with the Carrancistas during the revolution and was some kind of *general* or *coronel* for Carranza when the president came through here. Old Don Antonio was the one who really started all this. He was a bigger witch than anyone. He went to Veracruz and then Chiapas, and then he went to Mexico City."

The man Don Pedro was referring to was the father of Antonio Acero, the local *cacique,* a political strongman who still lived in Ahueta and owned the Finca El Rosal near Quetzalan. The son was a well-known politician and had been mayor of the county seat several times. His father controlled the coffee trade in the region for many years, amassing a huge fortune. I knew that old Don Antonio had been involved in the revolution, but not much more. His son was still widely feared in the area and was regularly involved in land-grabbing schemes and electoral fraud. His strong-arm tactics made him an important part of the ruling party's political machine. State governors and even national politicians all had their debts to the young Antonio.

"Old Don Antonio," Pedro went on, "came back here and took the *hacienda* at Ahueta with his army. He said that it was for the *presidente,* but I don't know. He became very rich. They said that he made a deal with the *talocanca* for the treasure in the mountain, and he was made a general. After being a Carrancista, he was a Villista, then an Obregonista, and his army kept everyone out of Ahueta."

Don Pedro seemed to think that there was something unnatural about old Don Antonio's amassed wealth, that he had made some kind of deal with the earth Lords. Pedro assumed that any man with that kind of power got it from the underworld and that the old man was a witch, or at least a potential witch. This was a common assumption. Probably, however, the old man had simply been a deft player in the strong-arm politics of the Mexican revolution, switching allegiances and applying force where necessary to further his economic interests at the expense of the local indigenous population.

"The old man had lots of men there at the hacienda, and they were all real *matones,* murderers. They would come into a village or a town and take what they wanted, all the pigs and chickens, then they would take people's daughters if they could find them. When those men came around, everyone went to their *cafetales* or their *milpas,* and some of the women hid in the caves and in the forest. Don Antonio's army just took what it wanted, and everyone had to give them what they wanted, or they got shot.

"Phoof! Splat! Dead!" Pedro exclaimed, illustrating the action with his fingers in the form of a gun shooting into the air. His forehead wrinkled, and his eyes widened. His lips tightened under his thin black mustache. He had probably fled those men several times. He obviously spoke from experience.

Pedro went on, "Well, Don Arcadio told me when I was a boy that Don Antonio one day sent all his men, the worst of them, out to the villages. They came here to San Martín, and they told all the men in San Martín to come over to see Don Antonio. They didn't know what Don Antonio wanted. They were all really scared. Most of the Cruzes and the Sandovals went into the mountains. They saw those men coming. There were a lot of them. The old man sent his troops over to get all the men from the village, the really important ones, the fathers and family leaders. Those *pistoleros,* his troops, shot anyone who wouldn't come along. They all went over to the Finca El Rosal at gunpoint, under guard. Don Arcadio, Don José Santos, Don Raul Sanchez, my uncle, and my father too, all went over there. They were just about the only ones who hadn't fled the town when those killers came."

With the exception of Inocente and Arcadio, those were the men in the picture with the horse that Don Pedro had just shown me. The photograph was taken at El Rosal and dated January 17, 1921.

"My father never told me about this because he was afraid of Don Antonio. He said that Don Antonio had a *tecuani,* a 'people eater,' for a *nagual* and that he ate Indians for lunch. If we were bad as children, he said he would send us to Don Antonio in Ahueta, and Don Antonio would have us for lunch, that is what he told us. He was really afraid of Don Antonio; he did not like him, not at all. Maybe that could be why he never told us much about him, but Don Arcadio did. He said it was how the witches started, how all the killing started.

"Well, all those men went up there to El Rosal, and they thought Don Antonio was going to jail them, or hang them, or maybe even eat them, Arcadio told me. They left the village late in the afternoon, and those *pistoleros,* all on horses, made them walk as fast as the horses ran. Everyone thought that they were going to be shot, or hanged.

"But when they got there, when they arrived at the gardens there, Don Arcadio said that El Rosal was like a palace. The gardens were full of flowers and more beautiful than in Quetzalan. There were lanterns and candles everywhere. They could smell good food and big pots of savory black *mole* sauce being cooked. Some of them were sure they were going to be eaten, but the others and his men said, 'Oh, no, Don Antonio wants to help you. He wants to take care of you. He wants to be your *patrón,* your big father.' There were lots of other men from San Andrés, San Miguel, Santiago, and all the other villages, too. They were all getting drunk. All the troops were already drunk.

"Don Antonio had fighting bulls there and fighting cocks too, they said. There was to be a great feast for everyone. Don Antonio's men took them all to a big room where they could stay. There was lots of *refino,* and there were women in printed dresses who served them there.

"Those women there, Don Arcadio said, were all there just for the men to take. They were waiting for them there, all those women who worked for Don Antonio. They were just waiting for the men to come to them. Good, ripe fruit they were. They were just waiting to be picked and pricked so their juices would start to flow. Everyone was drunk. It was really a *fiesta.* All the men, the men from the other villages and the men who worked for Don Antonio, said, 'Don Antonio is having a fiesta; he's having a party,' but the men couldn't leave.

"Don Arcadio wanted to leave. He did not like it there at all. He did not have much confidence in Don Antonio. He did not trust him at all. But Antonio's *pistoleros* said that he had to stay. Don Antonio wanted to talk to him tomorrow. Don Antonio wanted to see them all tomorrow. And those troops would shoot anyone who tried to leave, who did not respect, who did not honor, Don Antonio's invitation.

"The next day there were bullfights and cockfights, and Don Arcadio said that there was more *refino* than water there. Then there was a big feast there, plenty of *mole,* and rice and beans and tortillas for everyone. Don Antonio was in the big house, and each group of men was taken to see him, Arcadio told me.

"The *pistoleros,* his gunmen, came to each group of men and said, 'Don Antonio wants to see you; Don Antonio wants to see you, now!' And they took them to the room where Don Antonio was. Some of his *guardia* had rifles, and others had pistols, but they were all armed. They took the men up to the room where Don Antonio was seated. Don Antonio asked, 'Who are these? Where are they from?'

"'These are the ones from San Martín,' one of his men said.

"Don Antonio said, 'Tell them that I will make them rich, and tell them that I have many things for them. Tell them that they can have anything from my great store here,' and one of his men, who had a big book there, told them all that.

"'Tell them that there is much food and plenty of *refino* for them. Tell them that they may take what they want from my store there. Tell them that they will pay me with their coffee, that when they harvest their coffee they will bring it all to me in Ahueta. I want all their coffee, and they may sell it to no one else, or they will have no coffee,' he said, and the man with the great book told them that. He asked each man's name and how much coffee he could bring, Don Arcadio said.

"They were all taken to Don Antonio's store, and they were given bolts of cloth and hardware and machetes and cooking pots. They all took what they needed, and then they were taken back to Don Antonio. One man read a list of everything that they had taken to the man with the book.

"'Tell them,' Don Antonio told the man with the list, 'tell them I will give them corn and beans too, and rice for their coffee. Tell them they have to plant more coffee. Tell them they do not need to plant corn, that they do not need cornfields.'

"Don Arcadio said he did not like this, that he had not taken anything from Don Antonio.

"'How can we eat, how can we live?' Arcadio said he told the others there. 'Corn is our life. Corn is our blood. If we do not have our fields, how can we eat? What if Don Antonio doesn't bring in the corn, how can we live?'

"Don Antonio didn't hear him, or he would have had Arcadio's throat slit right there.

"'Oh, don't worry, Don Antonio is a good *patrón*,' the others all said. 'He will take care of us. He will pay us well for all the coffee we bring him. He is rich and will give us what we need for the coffee.'

"My father and my uncles all said that, Arcadio told me. They all thought that Don Antonio would process their coffee and give them corn and sell their coffee for them. He had told them to go to his store there and to take what they wanted and what they needed. He had told them that while they were there, they could eat what they wanted, and that there was *aguardiente* for them all, enough to get all of Quetzalan drunk. There were bullfights and cockfights, and these things were all for them, the men all said.

"'Don Antonio is a *patrón*, our Talocan *tatatzin*, our father the earth, an earth Lord,' they all said. But he was not like that at all. All those things weren't really just for them, Arcadio told me. Don Antonio was a big-time witch.

"Don Antonio's men wrote down all the things that had been taken. They put them in a big book that they had there, they kept accounts of everything, and when the men went home after three days there at the Finca El Rosal, they were told that they owed Don Antonio such and such amount of coffee. They all had to bring their coffee to Don Antonio.

"Don Antonio just wanted more and more coffee, Arcadio said. If he didn't get enough coffee from the people in the villages, he would steal it from anyone on the road to Ahueta. He just took the coffee from anyone else trying to take it out of the region; that way he had all the coffee.

"My father, Don Raul, Don José, and the rest of them all had most of their land planted in coffee, and Arcadio's family grew corn on the flat plains below the rivers. People traded coffee to the Cruzes for corn. They did not have much coffee, but they had the best land in the area. They had grown corn in those fields since the time before the present one, since the time of the tales of Juan Oso."

Juan Oso was a character from folklore who had become the local culture hero of the mythic past. Many of the tales of Juan Oso are suspiciously similar those of Quetzalcoatl, the feathered serpent lord-god of the Toltecs and culture hero of the Aztecs.

Pedro went on with his story. "Don Arcadio said he didn't take anything from Don Antonio's place. He was very careful not to leave with a debt to Don Antonio. He said he was the only one not to leave with a debt to Don Antonio. Don Antonio's men kept on saying, 'Take this. Take that, just take these things, and then you can give us coffee in return,' but Don Arcadio said that he had no coffee.

"'Well, plant some!' they all said, both Don Antonio's men and the men from the village. 'Don't be a fool, take these things, and then pay Don Antonio in coffee!' It was better to have Don Antonio give them things and pay for them with coffee than to have his men steal it, because that is what they were doing at the time.

"All the other men came back from El Rosal with lots of things. They owed Don Antonio much, and they brought him as much coffee as they could, but it was never enough for Don Antonio. They always owed Don Antonio more coffee than they had, and they began to tell Don Arcadio and the other Cruzes and the Sandovals, 'Let us use some of your land. Let us use some of your land that lies fallow,' but the Cruzes and the Sandovals would not let them use their land. Once coffee and the shade trees are planted, corn cannot be grown, not good corn at least.

"That was when the witches started to do evil things in San Martín, Arcadio told me. Don Antonio sent out the witches to see that there was plenty of coffee and that everyone was growing coffee for him. The first one who got it from the witches was Don Arcadio's aunt, I think, Doña Antonia Cruz.

"There was a lot of envy and jealousy here in San Martín when all those men came back from El Rosal, Arcadio said. The ones who got a lot of things wanted more land for coffee so that they could get more things from Don Antonio, and they asked the village elders to grant them land.

"Don Arcadio thought that my father and my uncles—all the Sanchezes—had made a deal there with Don Antonio and the witches, but I don't think that they did. My father was very afraid of Don Antonio and his *naguals.*

"Nobody liked the Cruzes. They wouldn't give permission for any more coffee to be planted on their land. That is what witches like, when there is dissension and discord. Everyone said that the Cruzes and the Sandovals were unjust.

"When nobody likes someone, and there is much envy, the Lords can be tricked. They might help a man who seeks something that is not just. When the witch presents his case to the Lords on his altar, he 'turns the candle upside down' and dreams. He asks the Lords to take his victim's *tonal.* So if we help the Lords with something 'a bit evil,' something savage, the Lords do not object. If something a bit evil should befall someone who is unjust, or who is not living well, it just brings them more food there in the earth. The Lords are happy to do this because this is their food, their sustenance.

"But if the witch has fooled the Lords, the one who was witched will later seek his own justice. The Lords will wait until the witch arrives, and then they hold a great trial in the underworld. The loser must serve the fires of the South, forever."

Pedro looked me in the eyes to see if I understood. I nodded.

"We all know the evil things the Lords can help our 'other self'—our animal, our *nagual*—do, but if the Lords don't think that it is justice that we seek, then nothing will happen. We ourselves are in danger of being kept in the world of dreams. Many times these things will not work, and they can kill the witch. Many witches have died like this.

"It was Don Antonio who started paying the witches to do foul things, to cause the 'shadow of death' and evil to come over the Cruzes. Arcadio's aunt, the first one that they got, was a widow, and she had a lot of land that she wouldn't let anyone use. Then the 'smoke of death' came over her. You know the smoke that those leaves, the ones we call the viper's leaves, produce."

Don Pedro was speaking of what was really the native equivalent of gas warfare. The leaves of the viper's vine are burned in front of someone's house, and the smoke is deadly.

"Don Antonio wanted all the land planted in coffee, and Don Arcadio's aunt would not let them plant coffee. She had no sons, and some of her nephews planted a cornfield or two for her. That was all she needed to live. She had no need to plant the rest of her land, but she would never let them plant it with coffee. She was unjust. Don Antonio knew that, and he paid a witch to get her. He wanted all of the land planted in coffee, and now it is. Antonio Cruz and Martín Sandoval still have a few cornfields down there, but it is almost all *cafetales* now.

"Arcadio thought that it was Don Antonio who started doing the evil things that happened, but I think that he just paid the witches off. That is what I heard. My father said that Don Antonio agreed with them that the Cruzes were not being just, and Don Antonio, I think, gave a witch some money so that something evil should happen over there to those Cruzes. He wasn't a witch, but he used the witches, all right. Somebody should have witched old Don Antonio, but they never did. He was too powerful. That was what Don Antonio did, all right. Maybe he was really the biggest witch of them all, the most dangerous witch.

"Those witches were potent ones then. They could kill a man just by looking at him. They could give him a 'bat hug' or a 'rabbit kick,' and that was it. Pow! Their lights were out; their candle was cut off. They could put their arms around a man like this with a 'bat hug,'" Pedro said, demonstrating how to grab someone at just about neck level from behind with both arms, just like Inocente had once shown me. "Then they'd pull them like this," he said, showing how to twist the arms. Snap! There are two or three shakes on the ground, and the lights are out," said Don Pedro, having just shown me again that very effective technique for breaking someone's neck, then watching death set in.

"Some of the witches even used the 'mule stomp' on their victims. They took the feet from a dead mule with horseshoes still on and knocked someone with them and then trampled them with those feet into little bits, to sausage meat, and tossed them down the ravine. It looked like the body had been trampled by a horse when they found it, but everyone knew it was really a witch.

"My father said that they used 'dog's gut' too, just a bit of a treated piece of dog's gut slipped into a taco or a tamale, and someone's whole gut would come out of them. They were dead in a day or two, if they lasted that long. Those witches knew their stuff. I've learned a few of their tricks, but not enough of them. I suppose you have, too, with all the time that you spent with Rubia and old Inocente, eh?" Pedro asked keenly.

"Yes, a few of them," I said, not wanting to let Don Pedro know just what I knew about witches and witchcraft. "They're all real killer's tricks too," I laughed a little bit.

"For sure," he agreed, and we began to arrange the altar for the curing that we were about to undertake. The Garcías would be arriving soon, I supposed, since it was already midafternoon. Amalia, Pedro's wife, brought out some food and admonished us both not to have too many *copitas* at the curing, or else we would be "cured," too, by the time that we finished. Don Pedro's *refino* was a particularly deadly *aguardiente* that he got from the hacienda at Ahueta, and I already knew quite well that it produced a monumental hangover.

Raul and María arrived with Linda and the whole family: José, his wife, and their three children, as well as his mother. María's mother, Don Pedro's cousin, Lilia Sanchez, and two of her daughters, María's sister and half-sister, also came over for the curing.

Linda and her two grandmothers were inseparable. Old María García and Lilia Sanchez were obviously close friends, and both doted on little Linda. While Don Pedro and I finished arranging the altar with the additional offerings brought by the Garcías and Sanchezes, the two old women patiently explained to Linda exactly what everything on the altar was.

As soon as the offerings of food, water, and flowers were properly placed, Don Pedro and I began our prayers. I lit the incense and then the candles. He prayed first, and I followed, lighting additional candles and dropping a few more grains of copal incense into the censer.

Then we asked Linda to stand before the altar, upon which we placed the pictures of her ancestors we had asked her to bring. Her two grandmothers came up to the altar to help the little girl explain to us who each individual in the photographs was.

"This is my grandfather, Miguel García," the little girl told Don Pedro and me, "with my grandmother, María." She continued looking up at her grandmother. "And there is his father in Quetzalan," she said, pointing to another photograph yellowed with age. "His father was called . . . what was his name, Grandma?" she asked Doña María.

"José," the old woman prompted.

Linda continued explaining who each individual was and, with some help, how they were related to her.

"Now then, my little one, you have a lot of ancestors here. Though they may rest in the Most Holy Earth," I said, stomping on the dirt floor, "we will ask them all to help us, to show us where your *tonal* rests, to help us restore it to you and make you whole again."

We gave Linda a bit of copal and told her to put it in the incense burner. Then I blew smoke all over her and let her go back to sit down with her grandmothers, who were gossiping away in the corner of the room. As usual during Nahua rituals, everyone was talking at once, paying little attention to the actual ceremony in progress.

Meanwhile, Don Pedro and I prayed in low tones that all her ancestors would help us to search out the lost soul of little Linda. Then Don Pedro prayed to the *patrones,* the patrons of our tradition of curing, who hold the earth and sky apart at the edges of the universe. He prayed to San Juan Lucero de la Mañana, Saint John Morningstar; San Juan Crecincia de Dios, Saint John Sprout of God; San Miguel, Salvador del Mundo, Saint Michael, Savior of the World; Santiago de las Estrellas, Saint James of the Stars; and others who have little to do with church ritual but a lot to do with the Most Holy Earth. Afterward, Don Pedro began to pray to Don Juan Manuel Martín, Don Miguel Martín Francisco, Manuel Martín Francisco, Juan Ocelotl, and Juan Antonio Abad, our predecessors who were the real patrons of the tradition. As he finished, I was thinking it was a very wonderful prayer. I decided to use it in the future.

We then sprinkled water from a bowl on the altar over everyone within range and added more copal to the censer. The dark, windowless room was filled with smoke and congenial voices as we took the bottle of *aguardiente* off the altar and began to pass it around. It was Don Pedro's most potent *refino*—close to straight alcohol.

Doña Amalia, Don Pedro's wife, had diminutive glasses set out, and she quickly snatched the bottle. She and María filled the glasses and began to offer them to everyone. Those little shots of *refino* were in fact far deadlier than just passing the bottle. With the bottle one could take as much or as little as one desired, which was convenient when it looked as if there would be toast after toast. But with the glasses, one had to finish each shot, leaving but a drop to be emptied onto the dirt floor as the Most Holy Earth's share.

We quickly finished the first bottle, and when José brought out another one, we finished that, too; by the time we said our last prayers, everyone was well inebriated.

The prayers over, Pedro once more had Linda's grandmother, Doña María, bring the girl up to the altar and told her to lie down on a *petate* mat that had been placed there. He then passed an egg all over her body. This was not a part of traditional curing, but I had seen Rubia use this trick with non-Indians. Pedro pressed very hard on the egg, causing the little girl to squirm and roll. Finally when he finished he took the egg and broke it into a dish on the altar. There was a stone inside it that he told Linda was what had been left in place of her *tonal* when she had fallen on a rock somewhere. (This trick is done by placing foreign elements high up in the hen's oviduct and letting the egg form around them. It is a particularly impressive trick and can, metaphorically, at least, help clients to realize that something has been removed from them and that they are ready to receive their souls back.)

Linda got up and went to listen to her grandmothers. Don Pedro took the cigarettes and hand-rolled cigars off the altar, leaving just five of each, and began to pass them around. María and her mother-in-law took the tortillas and the pot of beans from the altar and began to make little plates for everyone, adding a portion of savory stew that they had brought along. This was the first time that I had seen little Linda eat with relish. Her paternal grandmother went around telling everyone that Linda had made the stew and would one day make a good cook for someone. María and her mother sat talking with Linda, enjoying their light supper.

I could see that the little girl was beginning to be cured. Her grandmothers had given her a place in the household and taught her things that she needed to know. If only there was a way to keep this up in Mexico City, the little girl would indeed have her *tonal* back. If Raul could keep the job he had just obtained at the university and María continued cleaning with Marta, one of the grandmothers would become a necessity in the García household in Mexico City, especially now that they would be able to afford decent housing. That would solve a lot of problems for everyone, I thought, and this is what eventually happened in the García family. Raul's mother moved down to Mexico City just a few months later, much to Linda's delight.

The sun had long set, and I told Pedro that I would search for another dream that night. It was quite late, and I could see that there was far too much *aguardiente* flowing to stay any longer if I didn't want to stay the night. I bid farewell to Linda and her parents, telling them I would dream for the little one.

Don Pedro came outside the hut into the evening with me. The stars were out, and the night noises had already started. "It is time to search for a dream; that is what you must do," he said. "This little one almost has her soul back. If you can just find where it may be, then we can send the family out to make offerings and get it back. I, too, am sleepy and will see if I can find the little one's *tonal* in my dreams, but you have worked more for her than I, and you should be able to find it now. Remember the stone in the egg. I think that is where to look. Perhaps the 'hill hearts' have her *tonal.*"

The 'hill hearts' are those who look like us but come from the cave. They are the 'hearts' of the mountains, and their own 'hearts' are small, black, shining stones."

I handed over to Don Pedro the fifty pesos that we had agreed upon. It was an outrageous sum for assistance in curing, but well worth it to me. I was extremely happy with all he had told me about the War of Witches, and since Pedro had heard that Raul was working for the princely sum of twelve hundred pesos a month, nearly a hundred dollars, was sure he thought that I would pass on the expense. It was a small investment in their daughter's health, and Raul was now a rich man by village standards.

The García men came out of the house at that moment, probably to relieve themselves, and I bid them farewell again. As I got into the car to head off into Quetzalan, I was thinking above all about trying to make sense out of what I had heard about the War of Witches. There was a lot that Rubia and Inocente had not told me. Just what was their role in all of this, and what more did they know that they weren't telling me? This was a delicate matter.

THE NEXT MORNING I had to go back to San Martín to collect the Garcías before I could head back to Mexico City, and I also wanted to talk to Rubia, of course. Before leaving Quetzalan I stopped for some of her favorite sweet rolls, and this time, rather than take the car back over the rough trail to San Martín, I preferred to walk. The old cobblestone path wandered through the jungle and the coffee plantations on the way to San Martín. The morning was clear and bright as the clouds lifted over the hills just beyond the graveyard where I now knew the bones of my "friend" Arcadio rested.

That morning I resolved to confront Rubia about the War of Witches. I wanted to know what she knew about how it had started. Everything began pleasantly enough with coffee and my sweet rolls. Rubia wanted to know how the curing had gone. I still didn't know why she had not accompanied me to Don Pedro's, though his house was only a few hundred yards from hers. She had always gone with me to curings before. She never had got along very well with Don Pedro, I knew that, but as to why, I was not sure. Her first husband had been a Sanchez, like Pedro, but she later married a local schoolteacher who left her with five children early in the War of Witches.

I told her all about the curing and the dream of the night before, which was nothing spectacular. She told me I should go over to tell the Garcías anyway. Even though it wasn't important, it would at least show them that I was working on their daughter's problem. Rubia was quite pleased that both grandmothers had helped Linda to recall her ancestors.

"Those are the ones who will probably help you find the little one's *tonal* more than Don Pedro and all his prayers," she counseled me. "With just a few things, a few offerings for our mother, our father, the Most Holy Earth, the grandmothers should be able to get the little one's soul released.

"You tell Raul and María before they leave that the grandmothers should take Linda to the well down there and leave some things for all the ancient women of the West, the Lady of the Waters, and the Mothers of the Springs there."

"Of course," I replied, "that's just what our little dove needs her grandmothers for." I was beginning to see the wisdom of Rubia's ploy. The grandmothers were more a part of the solution than the mountain shrines of the "hill hearts" where Don Pedro had proposed that they go to leave offerings.

"Now what else did you hear over there at Don Pedro's last night before they all got drunk?" she asked me.

"Well, he told me a lot about the Cruzes, and he showed me some pictures. Did you ever know one of them called Arcadio Cruz?"

The glowing smile on her rugged face turned to an icy stare. "You figured it out, didn't you?"

"Yes. It was Arcadio Cruz I saw in the picture."

"I knew you would find out who that was. After fifty years Don Arcadio is the only one strong enough to still be there waiting for the Lords to catch the witch who got him. He still seeks justice after all these years. He won't just go away like a good *tonal.* What else did Pedro tell you?" she asked in a grave manner.

"He showed me a picture of your uncle with Inocente and some others at El Rosal, and he told me about Old Don Antonio from Ahueta. He told me that Don Antonio was behind it all, paying the witches to do their evil deeds, and how the killing started. It was Doña Antonia Cruz, he said, who was the first one to get it."

"Well, he got it all wrong," she said flatly. "He used to listen too much to Don Arcadio. Arcadio talked to everyone about it. His father sure wouldn't have told him that."

"What about the crucifixion?" I asked. "What happened there?"

If she was taken aback, she didn't show it. "Well, you'll have to find that out. They did it, all right. They hung old Martín Santos up, right down there," she said pointing to the churchyard. "It stopped those 'things,' those witches, but I wasn't there, or they might have gotten me too. I don't know too much about it.

"When it all started, when the witches really got going, there was no corn. There was no life in the village. The children of my uncle and my father, my younger brothers and sisters, were starving. Don Antonio offered them corn for their coffee. The Cruzes wouldn't give us any corn for our coffee. They didn't want it. They wouldn't even part with a measure of their corn. There were ones who died before Antonia Cruz—plenty of them. She was a tight old woman with much land that she would not use. There was no corn, and the people, the little ones, the children were starving. They were dying. There was no nourishment there. Our mother, our father, the earth did not give us enough for sustenance. The corn grew poorly in our *cafetales.*

"There was a witch, all right, but it wasn't old Don Antonio. It was down there with the Cruzes. There were people dying before Don Antonio began to give people corn for their coffee. Don Antonio was a big man, a great father, a *patrón,* but he wasn't a witch. He didn't follow the 'good path,' and he wasn't a witch. Maybe it would have been better if someone had shown him the good way, for he was a good *patrón.* He gave us corn—he gave my father corn, my uncle corn—and we could sustain ourselves. Don Antonio didn't start the killing; it was one of them down there, one of the Cruzes or one of the Sandovals. They stayed down there on their *milpas,* their cornfields, and wouldn't let anyone else have any corn. They wouldn't take coffee for the corn, and there were people in the village who suffered.

"My mother and her mother learned the way from the Totonacs who came to our house long, long ago, before the revolution. They learned that our father—our mother—there in the earth, was just. They learned how to ask for justice. They knew how to deal with a witch who was unjust, too. Others in the village did not follow the path, but they were witches just the same. My mother and her mother knew how to deal with them.

"The old woman, Antonia, got it, all right, but it wasn't a witch who got her. The Lords took her. They consumed her. She was unjust. She gave no one her land, the sustenance they needed to live here on the earth. It was then that the killing started. Pedro was right, but the witches were down there with the Cruzes, and it was they who sent the 'smoke,' 'the shadow of death,' and many other terrible things searching for us.

"Before you go back to Mexico City, you ask Pedro about the Cruzes and what they did here in San Martín. They got Pedro's mother-in-law and one of his aunts too. Arcadio was one of the good ones. He was married to one of Pedro's aunts, but they got him, too. Maybe Pedro knows something about what happened to Arcadio.

"Say nothing to Inocente about Arcadio Cruz, now that you know. That old man can still be quite dangerous," Rubia warned me. "Inocente always said that Arcadio Cruz was a witch, and if he knows that it is Arcadio that you see in Talocan then he may think that you're a witch, too. Maybe you could be out to do something a bit evil to the old man, that's what he will think, and then he is going to try to get you first. He is a very dangerous friend, my *compadre* is.

"You should go over there and see Don Pedro now, but be careful of what you say, and don't believe everything he tells you. There is much that he does not know about this matter, and about the path, too, that he should. Remember, he came from Puebla, not San Martín.

"You take care of the Garcías' problem first, then ask Pedro about these things," she told me.

Chapter 10

C R U Z

As I walked up to don pedro's house
I thought I was finally
getting somewhere,
but where?

I was finding out that there was no clear boundary
between witchcraft, healing, and social relations,
just as there seemed to be no clear path to "the truth,"
no single reality.

Everyone seemed to have his or her own ideas about the events of the twenties and thirties. Each villager had his or her own story, and as often as not their stories had little relation to one another. I was intrigued and gratified by Don Pedro's willingness to talk about the witches, but I had little idea about why he was doing it outside a desire to clear his father's name. It had been almost ten years since I had first come to the village, but I was just beginning to see the forces that had gone into shaping it.

Don Pedro was standing behind the counter of his general store when I came in. It wasn't even ten yet, but there were already a couple of drunks outside who, by the looks of them, had probably been quaffing down Don Pedro's *refino* since dawn.

"The light is upon us, good morning," I said as I entered.

"Good morning," Don Pedro replied. "Did you see clearly in the darkness?" he asked, meaning had I dreamed where little Linda's soul was.

"No, I didn't see much last night," I told him. "I went down a long river to a great pool. There were fish there, and then I crawled out into a garden with lots of flowers. I went back into the pool with the fish and swam down the river until there was a house. I stayed there at the house and then swam out of the underworld at the Great Water Mouth and woke up. That was about all I saw. Did you see things there that were clear?"

"Well, not much," he said, "but I was in the waters, too, a great pool. That just might be where the little one's soul is, not with the 'hill hearts.' I walked a long path and came to the great pool. I was very hot, so I went in and I stayed there. There were fish there, but no houses or villages. I came out at the Ahuetzic waterfalls."

"Maybe the little one lost her *tonal* in the waters, then," I said, remembering Rubia's solution to the problem. "Maybe we should have them leave some flowers and candles for the 'water ones' so that the little one's soul comes back."

"Well, it can't hurt them. Raul and María could take her down to the pool at Ahuetzic with some offerings."

"Perhaps it would be better if the little one went with her grandmothers," I suggested.

"Yes, perhaps it would," Don Pedro thought out loud, and then he yelled, "Pablo, come here!" to a boy out in the street. The boy came in, and Don Pedro spoke to him, "Do you know Doña Lilia Sanchez?"

"Yes," he replied, "she's the one who lives over near the Santos family."

"That's her. Would you go over and tell her that I would like to see her?"

"Sure," the boy replied and was off.

While the boy went to get Linda's grandmother, we talked about the dream and what kind of offerings they should take. Don Pedro was of the opinion that they should go to Ahuetzic to leave the offerings, but that was over twenty kilometers away, and I didn't know if the two old women could make such a walk. I suggested the town well, as Rubia had told me.

"Well, we'll see," said Pedro. "They're both strong old mules. They may just like the idea."

Finally Doña Lilia arrived. We explained the dreams to her and what we thought they should do. She seemed delighted and said that would give them a chance to stop in the market in Quetzalan. She was sure Doña María would go, too. She had to go home to get some things for market, she said, but then she would go right over to get Linda and her other grandmother. They would all go off to the waterfalls. Doña Lilia was perhaps already planning a picnic at the falls. Unfortunately this also meant that Linda would not be back until late afternoon or early evening, and it would be a very late night drive to Mexico City. Doña Lilia breezed out of the general store and headed up the hill to her house, leaving Pedro and me alone there.

"That just might work," Pedro said to me. "Those two old buzzards may just be the ones to help the little girl find her soul. She seems a lot better already."

"She sure seemed better last night here at your house than she was in Mexico City," I complimented Don Pedro.

"Well, maybe it was the prayers and the ancestors that did it. The little one is lucky it wasn't a witch that got her. If it was, we'd have a tough time getting her soul back."

"Yes, whatever happened to all those witches once the killing started?" I asked, seeing my chance to get Pedro back on the track of the War of Witches.

"We dare not say much about that here." He glanced around the store. "But maybe Juanita is in back and she can come here and wait on the customers," he said, pointing to the two drunks outside.

Pedro went back into the house and came back with his daughter Juanita, a plump little girl of twelve or thirteen years old who looked just like her father. He lifted the counter and ushered me into the house. We sat before his altar with all the offerings left from the night before. The flowers had wilted, and everything on the altar table except the votive candle was encased in solid pools of wax. Pedro offered me a short stool right in front of his altar, then he sat down facing the door so that he could see who was in the store.

"Can't say much about those things out there," Pedro began, "but if you want to know how the killing started, it started with Doña Antonia Cruz's death. When the old woman finally fell dead, there was no one who even wanted to go to the vigil. Her two brothers and old José Sandoval washed the body and laid her out with lots of flowers to help her on her way. There was no one who even volunteered to be a *compadre,* a sponsor, for the funeral. Usually everyone around here comes for a funeral, but for her, no one came. Some were too scared, and others just didn't like her.

They couldn't even find pall bearers for her." Pedro was right, everyone normally came to a funeral in San Martín. This was a very unusual situation.

"But the real trouble began before they had even planted the old woman in the earth. Her brother went up to Martín Sanchez, the *presidente municipal,* our mayor, as soon as she died and told him he was going to plant all of Antonia's land that year, since his sons were already farming part of it for her. Don Martín said, 'No, you have to go to Quetzalan for the deed to her land.'

"That wasn't the way things were done in town, because everyone had the right to that land. The Cruzes first, since they were her brothers-in-law, then the Sandovals, since she was a Sandoval, but my father had asked the town for the use of that land long before the old woman died, so he wanted part of it. Don Arcadio had helped him, and he had almost talked the old woman into letting him use the land when the witches killed her. There were others who wanted that land too. It was the best land near the town for cornfields, and everyone wanted it.

"Don Martín told them they had to go to Quetzalan for a deed. That was when the Cruzes and the Sandovals got really angry, Arcadio told me. The Cruz brothers, Arcadio's cousins, went over to see Don José Sandoval, and they all agreed that the land was theirs. The Sandovals and the Cruzes all got together. They all came up and threatened Don Martín with machetes, but he still said they had to go with a delegation to Quetzalan for a deed. Finally, they agreed. That was what got all the Cruzes and Sandovals together. Finally, that same day, they had enough of them to take the old woman up to the cemetery and plant her. There were not even enough of them to bury her until they found out about the land.

"They knew she had been witched. The body was already turning black after just a day or so, and they were sure it was Don

Martín, or someone he knew. Don Martín appointed Don Arcadio, Don José Sandoval, my father, and two others to go into Quetzalan to settle the deeds for Doña Antonia's land.

"The Cruzes and the Sandovals had some powerful witches down there. They were not at all like us. They did not follow the path, but they sure knew how to witch someone. They knew the 'shadow of death,' the 'evil smoke,' the 'viper's bite,' and a lot more, like the 'bat hug' and the 'jaguar's bite.' Old Inocente used that one a lot," Pedro commented.

"He did?"

"Sure did. He would take the teeth and get them right there," he said, pointing to two spots on either side of the jugular, "then rrrrip. They were done for." He showed just how, with both thumbs armed like that, the jugulars could be easily severed. The wound looked like a big bite, he maintained. I remembered the two sharp teeth Inocente had in his bundle attached to leather tubes. These probably fit right over his thumbs.

"The Cruzes and the Sandovals got together at the funeral for Doña Antonia, and they got the witches to go after Don Martín. Arcadio said that they brought the 'shadow of death' over the house of Don Martín, and I think that he was right. Both Martín's wife and daughter died that year."

"The 'shadow of death?'" I inquired.

"Yes, the 'shadow of death.' You know, where we go to the cave and get the earth there to bring the shadow, the darkness of the cave, over someone."

"No, I don't know much about that one. How do they do it?" I asked ingenuously, hoping that he would tell me something new about it. I knew that this involved the bat disease.

"Well, you just go into the cave, the Death Cave, or the other one down there, the Cave of the Evil Winds, and gather up the dirt.

You have to smoke a lot of cigarettes, though, so 'they' don't get you. You wrap up the dirt real well, then you take that to someone's house and leave it on the floor. The 'shadow of death' eventually falls over the house and takes someone away."

"It does?" I wondered again who could have given Rubia the bat disease. Or maybe it was an accident.

Pedro answered, "It sure does, but you never know who the shadow is going to fall on. Old Martín never got it, and sometimes the witch gets it, if the Lords don't like what he is up to." I couldn't imagine Rubia trying to kill someone.

Pedro went on in that same rapid voice, talking about those times as if I weren't there. I listened intently. "Arcadio went with my father, Don José, and the Cruz brothers to see about Doña Antonia's land. They all wanted it. There was no corn, or very little, and there were people starving. They went out to the forest and the *cafetales* to gather what they could, but without tortillas there just wasn't much to eat. Some of them went to Puebla and to Veracruz to work; others went to Mexico City. There were lots of bandits then, and they stole what they could. If someone was bringing in corn, or cooking pots, the bandits just stole them. Some of the bandits were old Don Antonio's men, but most of them were just people who didn't have anything. Don Antonio's men just stole the coffee, and he paid them for it.

"There was plenty of coffee, but no corn, Arcadio told me, that was why everyone wanted Doña Antonia's land. My father thought it would make a good *cafetal*, and Don Arcadio knew that the Cruz brothers couldn't use all the land. Arcadio told my father that he would help him get the use of that land if he planted corn, and my father agreed. My father was still going to plant a *cafetal*, though. He could get more corn from Don Antonio trading for coffee than the land would grow, he thought. Coffee was worth more than corn then.

"They all went into Quetzalan together, and my father agreed that the land was for the Cruzes, but that if they would let him plant corn, then he would farm part of the land. By the time they got to Quetzalan, they thought that they had an agreement that the Cruzes would get the land and let my father use part of it.

"My father went over to Don Antonio, his *patrón.* Inocente had told him that Don Antonio would help my father get the land that he needed. Inocente had talked to Don Antonio's men, and Don Antonio wanted to see my father. That was when Inocente started to work for Don Antonio as a *pistolero.*

"Don Antonio's men brought Inocente and my father to the big room there at El Rosal—the same one where the men had been taken before. Don Antonio sat at a big table where the man with the book had been, but the man with the book was not there.

"Don Antonio said to Inocente, 'Tell this man that he can have the land there if he will plant a *cafetal.* Tell him it is my land and that if he wants to plant a *cafetal* I will let him. I will give him the coffee plants, and he will plant it.' And Inocente told my father that.

"'Inocente,' Don Antonio said, 'now you go over with some of the men and see that no one goes on my land there. Don Pedro here is the only one who can go there.' Inocente did what he was told, and he told my father to go back to see the others, but not to tell them anything about what had happened at El Rosal. Inocente went out with those *pistoleros,* and they shot two of the Cruzes who were there. They were the nephews of Antonia who had been farming the land for her. Then Inocente and those *pistoleros* set up a camp there and kept everyone else off the land.

"My father went back to Quetzalan as he was told. He didn't know anything about the two Cruzes who had been shot by those men. He went with the others over to see Don Manuel Fernandez, the *presidente municipal,* in Quetzalan.

"Don Manuel told them, 'This land is Don Antonio's. He just bought it because the widow died and left it to no one. Unless you have a will, this land is for Don Antonio, and he has sent his men out there, so make sure you are very careful.'

"Don Arcadio and Don José were very upset, and the Cruz brothers were furious. My father didn't say anything. He told them there was nothing they could do. Don Antonio had guns, and he would kill anyone who came on his land.

"Now, that was when the killing really started! They all went back to the village and went to the Cruzes' house. Their two cousins were already dead when they arrived home. They were holding a vigil for them, a funeral. Everyone was there at the Cruz house, and they all were furious. Not only had they lost their land, but they had lost two boys as well. The Cruz brothers were going to get guns and go over and shoot the *pistoleros.*

"Arcadio told them that they were crazy; they would just get shot. 'Those *pistoleros* can't stay there forever,' he told them. 'Just wait.'

"Well, they were really mad. They found a witch who would get the *pistoleros.* Those men were not just, they told Don Arcadio, and he told my father. That meant they were going to have Don Antonio's men witched. They found a witch—Doña María Cruz— she was an evil old woman.

"My father told Inocente this, and Inocente went to see Don Raul, my uncle and Rubia's uncle. He told Don Raul that the Cruzes were going to witch the *pistoleros.* Don Raul told him how to protect himself and his men down there from the witches and Inocente let the *pistoleros* know that.

"Those men down there did not believe Inocente at first. They had guns and could kill any witch who came around. But the witches were already working. The longer those men, those *matones,* the *pistoleros,* stayed there, the more of them died. The snakes got them; the 'snake bite' worked well, and one of them got 'stomped up,' but they stayed there. They were ready, but not for witches. Finally they started to listen to Inocente and the things he learned from Don Raul, and not so many of the *pistoleros* died, because they were ready for the witches. They looked for the sticks in the brush, the ones witches put out to make the 'snake bite,' and they would not let anyone near the camp at night. Inocente learned from Uncle Raul what the witches did, and he stopped them, all right, but he didn't stop them in town.

"'We will have to get those men,' the Cruz brothers said, but Doña María's witchcraft was not working on the *pistoleros* anymore. They thought it was Don Martín who was after their land, and after the 'shadow of death' didn't work, they had old María ask the Lords to take him away. They said the *talocanca,* the servants of the Earth who live in the cave, 'got' him. They found his horse near the Earth Mouth, and no one ever saw Don Martín again. 'They' grabbed him and took him into the cave, I am sure.

"This made all the Santoses and Sanchezes really mad, and they went after the Cruz brothers and José Sandoval. Don José Sandoval got it from a jaguar, and the Cruz brothers both were found dead in their cornfields from the 'snake bite.'

"I think it was Inocente that got them," Pedro said, "or maybe it was my uncle Raul. Raul learned those things from the Totonacs when he was a boy as Rubia's mother did. The Totonacs were the ones who showed their mother the path, but it was Don Raul who really knew how to ask the Lords for justice." Pedro looked out the open door into the general store and got up for a moment to see how his daughter was doing. Everything seemed all right, and he returned to his low stool.

"Inocente was a foul one, and a dangerous one, then, but he became even worse and more dangerous," Pedro resumed. "Inocente was a *pistolero* then, but Uncle Raul taught him how to do those same things without a gun. Inocente lived down there on that land for three years with the *pistoleros*. Arcadio was wrong; they didn't just go away. They were terrible. They just took what they wanted. They even came to our house, and my father gave them anything that they wanted, or they would have shot him.

"Finally, after three years, they said, 'Don Pedro, come down here and start to clear the land for a *cafetal*,' and my father went down there with us to start clearing the land. The Cruzes were really angry. They sent an evil wind that got my sister. She died even before she got back to the village, and my father was so sad that he quit clearing the land and planting coffee bushes. But the *pistoleros* told him that they would come and kill him if he didn't continue, and we all went back down there. They stayed there to make sure no one destroyed the coffee or shade trees.

"Inocente was the chief *pistolero*. He was the worst one. He married my uncle's wife's cousin and brought her down there to the *cafetal*, but she preferred life in the village, so she was always in town and Inocente then came up here to live, too. Everyone was afraid of him but my uncle Raul. He and Raul were good friends. With Inocente and Raul there, the witches couldn't get those *pistoleros* anymore, and the *pistoleros* took more land from the sons of the Cruz brothers. Raul and Inocente sent Martín Santos down there to plant *cafetales*. The Cruzes were going to get him, but Don Raul protected him. Inocente was a much better witch than a *pistolero*, and he was much more effective too. When he and my uncle witched someone, they were goners. Dead! Out!

"Doña María Cruz was the biggest witch down there. Everyone knew that she had had Don Martín taken away to the cave. They all wanted to get her and cut off her candle, but Inocente and my uncle Raul didn't know how and Rubia's mother couldn't either. Finally a young woman who was just learning these things from Rubia's mother had a way to do it. She made some of the things we call the 'flowers of Talocan,' and one day at mass on the saint's day she put one of them on Doña María, right there at mass. Doña María turned and stared at her and gave her the 'evil eye.' It was so powerful that the woman died within a week, but Doña María was dying too. Her *tonal* was covered by the 'flower of Talocan,' and the fat old woman only lasted about two more weeks.

"I don't know what she did to the young woman, but it could have been the 'rat's bite' or the 'buzzard's claw' and not an 'evil eye.' You know, with those things you just have to prick someone and they're dead. Some of the witches used to carry those things with them. They would put them in a belt or in a bag, and no one knew they were there. When I was a boy, my father always had something like that with him. They said those things were better than guns because no one knew what they were. The *autoridades* couldn't catch you then.

"After María Cruz got it, there weren't many more deaths for a while. She was the big witch. There were a couple of witches with the Sandovals, and the Cruzes—the ones that were still left. They knew a few witches in Yohualichan, the village down the hill, but they didn't follow the same path as we did. We learned from the Totonacs. Maybe they learned from the Totonacs, too. There were a lot of Totonacs down in Yohualichan.

"By this time the Cruzes didn't even plant much corn on their land down there anymore. Don Antonio paid everyone with so much corn for their coffee that there was too much corn. No one knew what to do with all their corn, so they sold it. Didn't get much for it, though.

"Don Arcadio helped arrange for the Cruzes to let others plant *cafetales* on the land that was not being used, and our *cafetal* where the *pistoleros* were began to give us a lot of coffee. Inocente's men helped us pick the coffee, and two of them, Pablo and Manuel, married Santos girls. Ismael was one of the *pistoleros,* too, who worked for Inocente. So was Ignacio. He married a girl up at the end of town. Finally none of them were living down there on the land; they all had houses here in the village. They all had their own *cafetales.*

"Inocente did not even carry a gun anymore. He had better ways to get someone than with a gun that he learned from Uncle Raul. He could give someone the 'evil eye' or the 'breath of death'— just blow on them, and they were as good as dead. Everyone knew that, and no one would bother Inocente anymore."

"Was that the end of the killing?" I asked Don Pedro. I figured that this was about the late twenties, and there was no mention of the crucifixion yet or the end of the war. By this time the economic situation had obviously changed, and coffee was the mainstay of the economy. The town seemed to have become rather prosperous, mirroring in a small way the coffee boom days of Quetzalan, when the cathedral was begun. To a certain extent, my research in the town archives had told me, a money economy had supplanted subsistence corn agriculture. This change was something that old villagers had talked about freely. It was only the witchcraft that they were reluctant to disclose. Checking further in the town records to see if there was a lull in the killing, however, would be very difficult, as they were in total disarray.

I knew that there was more to this story than I had heard up to this point, and I wanted to keep Don Pedro going. I wanted to see if I could get some more information about the crucifixion and the final resolution of the war of the witches.

"What happened to all the witches?" I prodded him.

It was already early afternoon, and Doña Amalia was back from Sunday market in Quetzalan. She entered the compound from the back gate, set her huge pack down in the cookhouse, and came out into the main room of the house where I sat with Don Pedro.

"Well, what have you been doing all morning? Getting lit again, after last night?" she asked.

"No, not a drop," I replied. "Don Pedro has been telling tales." I didn't want to say about what.

"You mean he didn't even offer you a *copita?*" She reached for a bottle of green *yolixpa* that was on the altar behind me, poured two little glasses, and offered them to us. "This'll warm your heart and light up your tales. I'll get some things for a few tacos. Juanita didn't get you anything?"

"No, she's been in the store all morning," I replied.

Doña Amalia went back out to the cookhouse and began putting her purchases away, leaving Don Pedro and me alone in the main room again.

"Come on, tell me what happened after Doña María got it."

"Well, not much happened after she got it—not for a while at least. She was the big witch for the Cruzes. They knew some people from Yohualichan, as I said, who knew how to do evil things, but they weren't too bad. There was some sickness that everyone said was done by them, but not much else until Martín Santos's son got it.

"It was Arcadio's son and another of the Cruz boys who got him. They waited for him down in the ravines with machetes. They hacked him to pieces and buried him there in the ravine. Nobody ever would have found him if it hadn't been for Pablo, who was out hunting at the time. Pablo was one of the *pistoleros* who worked for Inocente. He married in town and lived on the road to Quetzalan. He was down there when they buried the boy. He dug him up and took him to Quetzalan to Don Manuel Fernandez. He didn't tell Inocente or anyone in town; he just went there. Pablo was not a Sanmartino.

"Don Manuel sent out the police, and they got the two boys on the road to Quetzalan. They jailed them. No one knew what happened to them there, and they hanged them two days later. Then Don Manuel came to town and caused a lot of trouble. He had the mayor and the judges arrested for not doing their duty. The Cruzes were furious because no one had told them about the boys' arrest, so that they could pay to get them out. They just hanged those boys there in Quetzalan. They strung them up on the scaffolding out there at the end of town and pushed them off. Thwomp! Dead!

"Arcadio's son was just a little older than I was. I used to hunt with him and harvest coffee with him. I don't know why he went after Pepe, Don Martín's son, but it might have been because of his sister. Pepe was older, and he was looking for a wife. He was interested in young Arcadio's sister—maybe he did something to her, maybe he had her in the cornfields down there, I don't know. When she heard they had hanged her brother, Elena became very ill. Don Arcadio was sure that Martín had hired a witch to get his daughter.

"The Santoses were furious, of course, because their son had been hacked up, but Don Manuel wouldn't even send the body back to town, or what was left of it. They buried him there in Quetzalan before anyone here even knew he was dead. He had no ancestors there, and he would never find his way home on the Day of the Dead. He was buried with the bones of strangers. They couldn't even hold a proper vigil or funeral for him. For many years, they said he walked the graveyard there in Quetzalan with the boys they hanged there, the ones who murdered him. They were all trying to find their way back to San Martín. People were really scared to go by that place at night. Some people even saw the boys there. All three boys were looking for Sanmartinos to take them home.

"That was when the witches started to do their evil deeds again. Inocente had gone to Quetzalan about the same time, and the

Cruzes were sure Pablo had told Inocente about the murder before he left, but he didn't. They thought it was really Inocente who had the boys picked up and hanged. Don Arcadio was really angry. He said that Inocente was the biggest witch in town, even worse than my uncle Raul. Don Arcadio found a witch to send an evil wind that got Inocente's wife. That was just after Lucas was born, and he almost died without a mother, but his aunts took care of him and he became strong.

"Inocente and my uncle decided that the Cruzes had to be stopped, and they did some pretty bad things. There were six of the Cruzes who got it then, even the little ones, the children. Then the Cruzes got my aunt, Raul's wife, and the killing really started in earnest.

"Inocente's daughter, Lucas's sister, got it. She was one of the most beautiful girls in town. She was a gem, a precious little one, but they got her too.

"Well, old Inocente was furious, and he got the daughter of Manuel Sandoval—a shame she got it. He stomped her to hamburger and threw her in the ravine here in town. It was Inocente who did it. I saw him coming back with blood everywhere. He went over to my uncle's—they were two men without women, and my mother helped out and cooked for them. Those two witches thought of nothing but how to do their evil deeds. That's what my father said. He knew how to do some of those things, but those two, well, they were really dangerous.

"Inocente and my uncle did more and more evil things then. The Cruzes did horrible things, too. For three years they went on killing one another. One was witched, and then another was witched. There were so many people being witched that no one knew, none of us knew, who was going to be the next one. I was really scared. Everyone was getting it, especially the children; they are the weak ones who don't hold their souls well. There were a lot of children who got it. One and then another." Don Pedro was beginning to become upset. His voice had become high pitched and strident.

"Rubia's mother tried to stop them," he continued, catching his breath a bit. "She was with Inocente all the time, and she wanted them to stop the killing, but her brother and Inocente wouldn't stop. The Cruzes and the Sandovals did the same kinds of things, and there were a lot of people who got it. Rubia's mother wanted the killing to stop, and she went to Don Arcadio. She told him that they had to stop the killing, and he came up to see my uncle and Inocente. He wanted them to stop, but they wouldn't. That was when Rubia's mother got it. One of the Cruzes got her. They brought the 'rain of the underworld' down on her when she was there.

"That was a very bad time in the village; no one would pay for our coffee. Don Antonio didn't give as much corn as before for the coffee, and there was much starvation. The people had only what they could gather from the forest and not much else. Inocente did all right because Don Antonio paid him, but no one else was doing very well.

"Then Arcadio got it. They got him forty years ago yesterday, April 5, 1937. My father insisted we go to the *velada,* and Rubia went, too. My father was his *compadre de la cruz* for the funeral. We kept his name alive, even in Puebla, for seven years after Arcadio was consumed by the earth. Everyone else said that was really dangerous, that the Cruzes were going to witch us too, but my father was Don Arcadio's *compadre.* We went with flowers and incense, but I was really scared. My uncle said they would eat us down there at the Cruz house, but they didn't."

"Was that when it ended?" I was stunned. How could all this have happened here?

"No, not then, but it wasn't long before they hung old Martín up out there in front of the churchyard."

At that moment Doña Amalia came in with two plates of beans and a large cloth filled with homemade tortillas. "You been talking about those witches again, eh, Pedro?" she asked, looking at him closely. "You were lucky you went to Puebla. You'd have been dead too. That uncle of yours was sure a mean one," she commented as she put the food down for us.

"Now have something to eat, and don't talk about those 'things.' They were evil and dangerous. You're just lucky there are no more witches here."

Chapter 11

THE WAR OF WITCHES: THE END

LINDA AND HER GRANDMOTHERS
HAD STILL NOT RETURNED
BY THE TIME WE FINISHED EATING
AT THE SANCHEZ HOUSE.
I bid Don Pedro farewell and told him
I was going to see Rubia. If anyone from
the García family came by,
I was ready to leave for Mexico City.

Pedro's long description of the war of the witches had left me speechless. The tale was fantastic but probably quite accurate. After lunch I retreated up the hill to the edge of town. There was a high rock outcropping above a cornfield that belonged to the Sanchez family where I often went up to think when I was in the village. From this spot I could see the whole Sierra, its high mountains and deep valleys dotted with little white villages and stone churches. The land was crisscrossed with cornfields and coffee gardens, and the clouds imposed an ever-changing pattern of color on the patchwork landscape.

I began to furiously scribble notes while I sat there and contemplated the Sierra: the names, the dates, and what had happened. I could not envision what it would have been like growing up then. I tried to imagine the predicament of the villagers. Was it justice that had been sought from the Most Holy Earth, or was it vengeance that had motivated the War of Witches? How did it end? What was the real story of the crucifixion? The survivors—Rubia, Pedro, and Inocente—did not seem satisfied by the Earth's justice. No wonder they didn't seem to want to talk about these things. They had known one another for seventy or eighty years. That alone was beyond me—I was then twenty-eight. So it was my eager curiosity, as well as my emotions, that drove me to seek more answers and to disturb those memories where they had rested so long.

As I walked all the way down the hill, I could see Rubia sitting on the stoop, her long white hair in a single braid down her back. She was looking down the street toward the churchyard and didn't see me approaching.

When I got close enough for her to hear me, I announced, "Good afternoon, our little grandmother."

"Aye! You're going to scare the soul right out of me. What do you come around like that for to scare a poor old lady? Now what do you want?" she asked curtly.

"Well, the Garcías aren't back yet, so I thought I would stop to talk."

"Got bored with Don Pedro, eh?"

"Not really. He told me a lot about 'them.'"

"Did he tell you what really happened, or another pack of lies?"

"I don't know. I thought maybe you could tell me."

"Well, not here, I can't. Let's go inside," she said, propping herself up with her cane. With great effort, she made her way into the house and sat down at the big table in front of her altar.

"Lupe!" she called out. I could hear Lupe and a friend in the kitchen. "Is there any more coffee?"

"Of course, Grandmother."

"Well, bring us two of them. Now what did Don Pedro tell you about all this time?"

"Well, he told me about all the killings, the Cruzes, and the Sandovals. He told me Inocente lost his wife to 'them,' and that your mother tried to stop it and then 'they' got her. It must have been terrible then; was that how it all ended, how they got rid of all the witches? What happened to them all?"

"Well, they're all either gone, or dead," she said, pausing.

"But what happened, Doña Rubia?"

"Well, as I said, I can't tell you. I wasn't here when they hung up Martín Santos on the cross down there in the churchyard."

"Where were you then?"

"We were at El Rosal. Inocente found us a place to stay there at Don Antonio's. It wasn't safe here. They had already taken my daughter and my mother and Inocente's wife and his daughter. Lucas came to stay with us, and he was like one of my boys. Inocente had no one to take care of him, and my husband, my old man, had long since disappeared. He split out of here when the first witches were getting it. He thought my uncle was going to get him. He wasn't from here, you know. He was a teacher. He didn't want to hear about the witches, but when he saw everyone dying he got scared. And when he found out that Uncle Raul and my mother were involved in the witchings, then he left. He didn't want anything to do with what was going on here in San Martín."

"How long were you at El Rosal?"

"It seemed like a long time—about three years, from the time that my mother died until about a year after they hung up that old Santos witch. By that time all the witches had gone, and no one would do that kind of thing anymore here in town. They were all afraid. Uncle Raul had gone to Puebla with Pedro's mother while they waited for his father to get out of the calaboose. All the other witches had left town, too. There were no more witches then." She looked pensively at her altar, eyeing first the pictures on the wall, then the offerings, and finally the trunk below, where, like Pedro, she kept things of her forebears.

Was she thinking of all those consumed by the earth, perhaps?

"After Inocente's wife got it," Rubia went on, "I knew that things were getting bad there in the town. Inocente had the two children, and they were here more than they were up at his house. So was he. My mother spent a lot of time with Inocente and Uncle Raul. When my daughter had the 'shadow of death' come over her, Mother insisted that I learn to dream, too. I knew all her prayers and things, but I didn't know how to get around in dreams. She and my uncle helped me find that bright little hummingbird that always led me."

This was the first time that Rubia had mentioned what her own *nagual* really was. She apparently felt no fear of revealing this deepest secret to me. She must have been confident that I was not about to embark on a career of witchcraft.

"But my little one, little Marta, died anyway. It was a witch, and I could do nothing about it."

Rubia was getting way off the track of her story. This wasn't the way she usually told a story, and this was obviously not a story that she had told before. It was coming in bits and pieces, fragmented and disconnected. This was not a story that was easy for her to tell. I thought a few well-placed questions might help.

"What did your mother do then to stop the witches?"

"Mother said that the witchcraft had to stop. At Marta's vigil she told Inocente and Uncle Raul that she was going to go down to the Cruzes and the Sandovals to talk with them. There had been enough people killed here in San Martín.

"Uncle Raul especially was furious that she did that. He said they were going to get her if she went down there, but Mother insisted. It was just after Inocente's daughter got it, and my little Marta. They all said that my mother would bring back an evil wind, or a bad air of some kind. She went down there anyway, and with Arcadio's help she implored them, she beseeched them, not to ask the Lords for more deaths. The Lords of the earth had eaten enough Sanmartinos, she said. They didn't need any more. Justice had been done, and to ask the Lords for more, she said, would only anger them. They had probably tired of eating Sanmartinos and would be angered by everyone constantly asking them for more and more help on this earth.

"Arcadio agreed, and he came up to talk to my uncle. My uncle was the one no one would go after. He had many, many animals, and they were all dangerous. He's the one who taught Inocente 'the path.' Inocente didn't know half what my uncle did, but Inocente was still very angry about his wife and daughter, and so was my uncle. Inocente's daughter, little Alicia, had been like his own. They were not about to stop, they told Arcadio. They had done nothing. They had asked the Most Holy Earth for justice. They wanted justice, and the Most Holy Earth would give it to them."

"Did you hear all this? Did you see all this?" I asked Rubia.

"Of course I did. Arcadio stayed with us while he and my mother begged them to stop. Arcadio pleaded with them for days, but they just thought he was afraid of them. My mother pleaded with them too, but they thought that she was foolish going to the Cruzes and the Sandovals. It was the Lords, they both told her. They were seeking justice. No one could do more than help the Lords to seek justice. They followed the way. The Most Holy Earth and the ancestors give us the only justice needed here on the earth, they said.

"They helped the ancestors a lot, though. Those two knew better than anyone how to help the Lords, and they did, they sure did. My mother knew what they did and so did Arcadio, so did Pedro's father. When they asked the Lords for justice, they got it."

"Well, what happened to your mother?" I asked.

"I think it was the 'rain of death' that got her. She was out in the rain, and then she was all covered by sores, and she was bleeding everywhere. We tried to care for her, but there was nothing we could do. Inocente wouldn't even come to the house to see her. They had been together often since his wife had died, and she took care of him and the boy more than even I did. Lucas was staying with us, but Inocente wouldn't even come to the house until after Mother died.

"He came for her vigil, her funeral. When she died, I didn't know what to do, but I didn't want to stay in the town. I was sure they would get me, or one of the boys. Inocente said there was a house at El Rosal, and we all went there, Inocente too. He thought maybe he would get it next. But Inocente came back here to town and stayed with my uncle often. He and my uncle really knew how to do some evil things. We were glad to be away from San Martín at that time.

"There were too many people dying, and there was not enough corn for the coffee everyone grew. I bought and sold things in the markets—guavas and peppers—and took things to Zacatlan and Tlapa. Sometimes people there in Quetzalan, or in San Andrés, would ask me to cure, so I did that too. Don Antonio still paid Inocente. Don Antonio and Dr. Rosas in Quetzalan insisted the boys stay in school, so they helped us with things. They both became *compadres.*"

Rubia then began another long digression about the time she had spent at El Rosal and the education of her sons, all but one of whom had become rural schoolteachers. Another question got her back on track.

"What about Don Arcadio?"

"When we left for El Rosal, Arcadio was already dying. It was the same 'evil rain' that got my mother. We came back for the *velada.* Everyone thought my uncle did it, and I suppose they were going to get Uncle Raul, but he was just too strong. They couldn't get him, and they couldn't get my *compadre* Inocente, either. He and my uncle were the ones the Cruzes and Sandovals really wanted. No one could get them, but there were others that they got.

"Don Pedro's grandmother got it. They all thought that Pedro's father was a witch. He wasn't like Uncle Raul and Inocente, though. He didn't have many animals. My mother and Uncle Raul had taught him 'the path' and how to dream. He was a curer, but not a witch, I think. He always told my mother he didn't like what those witches did. He was the *mayordomo* for San Martín, and then he was the *presidente municipal,* our mayor. That was why they hauled him off to Puebla. They said that he was responsible for not stopping the crucifixion."

"Good afternoon," a woman's voice called from outside the front door. It was Doña María, Raul's mother. I wondered where Linda and her other grandmother were. Doña María had dressed in her finery for the visit to the shrine and a stop at the market at

Quetzalan. She had on strands of bright red beads and her finest gold earrings. Her dark, withered face was crowned by green and violet wool wound up into her hair and covered by her finest white lace *quechquemitl.* It was hard to imagine her walking twenty kilometers wearing all that.

"Ah, it is our honored little mother. Please come in. Lupe, is there more coffee? You have been to the market?" Rubia asked.

"Yes, on our way to pay the 'water ones' to bring us little Linda's soul," Doña María said.

"Well, what was there at the market today? I didn't go myself, but Lupe did." The two old women started to discuss in detail prices, quantities, qualities, along with who was there. I really did not want to listen, so I excused myself and said that I was going to go to Quetzalan and would return to San Martín to go with Linda and her parents back to Mexico City.

As I was leaving, Doña María asked, "O sir, may I follow your path to the city?"

"Of course, my honored little mother," I replied. I was delighted. Her grandmother could do far more good for Linda's soul than I ever could. Rubia flashed a knowing smile, and I could see that she, too, was delighted that Doña María was going to go back with us to Mexico City.

As I was walking, I kept thinking about the War of Witches and what I had heard, but there was still one thing I really didn't know much about: the crucifixion. I had hoped to find out more about that from Rubia. I was sure she had heard every detail from the local gossips, even though she had not been living in the village at the time. Was it embarrassment or sadness, or town politics and the role that her family had played that had stopped her from telling me about this? What could have led them to crucify a witch?

By the time I arrived in Quetzalan, packed my things, and paid my bill, it was dark and raining. Driving over the tortuous trail to San Martín, I was still thinking about the witches. There was something very strange about the disembodied responsibility that witches and curers felt for their actions, and I could feel some of the disconnection in myself, too, when I healed. The Most Holy Earth was at once the Land of the Dead and the source of life. As the ancient Aztecs sang in time of famine,

> Oh, the fruits of the earth, the green and growing things
>   have gone,
> they have hidden themselves away!
> O Lord, Our Lord, Lord of Tlalocan, O Provider!
> What does your heart will?

As I crawled over the ruts in my car and came around the sharp curves in the darkness and rain, the headlights would catch an animal scurrying for the brush or a dark figure leading a burro heavily overladen with firewood. There were strange images and half-images I saw from a past that was not really past, here on the way to San Martín. As I pulled into the village, there were only a couple of lamps and few other signs of the twentieth century.

I wound my way up the hill to the Garcías' house and stopped. It would be at least a five-hour drive to Mexico City, and probably more in this weather. Getting out of the car, I struggled with my umbrella and lit a cigarette. Perhaps I should have stayed in Quetzalan and started off early in the morning.

"Good evening," I called out as I approached the door.

"Good evening," said Raul, Linda's father, from inside. "Where have you been? We have been waiting."

"Didn't your mother tell you I went for the car?" I asked, shaking off my umbrella and puffing on the cigarette so that there was plenty of smoke to keep any mischievous supernaturals away at night.

"She is not here."

"Well, I saw her at Rubia's a while ago and told her I was going for the car. Is she still there?"

"She must be," said Raul. "Maybe Pepe, José's son, can go get her. Lilia has made us some *gorditas* and *tlacoyos* to take along. Just let me get our things, and we are ready to go."

Raul had two huge sacks that completely filled the back compartment and the front trunk of my newly acquired Volkswagen bug. I could see that this was going to be a long and slow trip back to Mexico City with five people and all of Raul's cargo.

María and Linda were ready to go. José offered Raul and me a small glass of *yolixpa* while we waited for his mother to return. He wasn't pleased that his mother was going to the capitol, and he told me so. He said the old woman had never been as far away as Zacatlan and told Raul that he should take good care of the old woman. Raul assured him that he would and that his other brothers would, too. Mexico City would be just like being at home, he told José. Maybe even better, I thought.

Finally Doña María arrived. She went into the house, removed her Sunday finery, and put a few things in an old sack. She put all that in a pack held by a heavy brown tumpline around her head as if she were set to go to market or for a long walk to the *cafetales*.

"You don't need that, mother," Raul said. "Don Timoteo has his car here. The little red one right there."

"Oh, that's how we're going. I thought maybe the priest had left the car there." Padre Guillermo, the town priest, also had a red car, but of a different make. For Doña María, a red car was a red car.

Doña María, Linda, and her mother, María, piled in the back, and Raul sat up front with me. We bid farewell to everyone and took off through the dark, misty rain. It was a very slow ride to Quetzalan with the car fully loaded and steamy with the windows rolled up. Raul and I talked about his new job with the university and how much better it paid than harvesting coffee. People who picked coffee were given a place to stay, which was often little more than a lean-to or a shack, and a few pesos for each hundred-pound bag of coffee that was delivered.

As we were making our way up the switchback curves to Zacatlan, I could hear Doña María starting to get sick. She began throwing up. The rain had stopped, fortunately, and I opened the windows, but it didn't help the smell. I could feel myself starting to gag. Finally I found a spot to pull over, and we all got out for a breath of fresh air. Raul and I cleaned up the backseat as best we could, and then, putting a poncho down on it, he got in, leaving his mother the front seat.

This was worse for her. I could see in the lights of the on-coming traffic rushing at us that her eyes were wide with terror and her knuckles were white where she held on to the Volkswagen's dashboard. This was definitely Doña María's first car ride. I tried to talk to her, to soothe her, but all the way up to Mexico's central plateau she said nothing and just held on.

We stopped in Oriental, on the way to the city of Puebla, for gas. Doña María had obviously never seen a gas station, either. She got out of the car, walked a few meters and squatted down to urinate, the vast folds of her skirts providing ample privacy.

I said nothing, but the attendant commented with disgust, "Indians! Those Indians."

I bought some *atole,* a corn gruel that was very soothing to the stomach, and a soda from a small all-night restaurant and took it to

Doña María in the hope that it would calm her twisted insides. She finally smiled as she began to blow on the hot liquid. She said that she had some *gorditas* in her things, so I opened the trunk and got them out. We nibbled on them under the cold white lights of the PEMEX sign in the clear chill of the highlands. She confided to me that she had never been so far from the village and asked if there was much farther to go. I said that there was, and we climbed back into the car. Everyone else was soon asleep as we drove through the brightly lit industrial zone, at the beginning of the long flat Valley of Oriental.

Doña María, however, couldn't sleep. She kept up a nervous chatter, asking questions about one or another of her relatives who lived in Mexico City. Finally, by the time we arrived at the toll road to Puebla, I felt it might be the right moment to ask her if any of these relatives might be related to the witches. Questions about witchcraft were not something that I could approach her with directly. It had to be done in a roundabout way.

Finally, after several attempts, she gave me the standard reply that I was used to: "Well, once there were many of those 'things.' But they are all gone now."

"What happened to them?" I asked.

She looked back, probably to make sure that everyone was asleep. "They all killed each other, or they left town."

"Why?" I had little hope of getting her to say any more about the matter.

"Because finally they hung one of them up on a cross. It was my uncle, Martín Santos. That scared all the witches away."

"Was he a witch?" I asked, shocked by her sudden directness.

"Sure was," she replied, "and the Sandovals got him. Martín Sandoval, who used to be the dance master for the Santiagos, got him."

The Santiagos were a local dance troop that performed the medieval dance-drama of Saint James at local festivals. The Sandovals had been the organizers and masters of the dance for generations because they possessed the earliest copy of the play in the village. Sometime in the 1920s, however, when the Sandovals no longer had enough money to finance the festival, Manuel Sanchez bought a copy of the text from a man in another village and formed his own dance troop. This left the Sandovals extremely angry.

"How did that happen?" I asked. "How did they get him?"

"Well, one of the Sandoval sons got it. They said someone gave him a 'tiger bite' right in the neck outside his house at night. They ripped his throat out. They left him there. The boy had no more blood. He was dry. They said that was the work of a witch. Raul and Inocente were gone; they had left town. Those were the two who did those things—everyone knew that—but they weren't anywhere in town. Don Martín Sandoval was furious. First he talked to the Sandovals and the Cruzes, and they were going to get a witch to get those two, but Martín wanted all the witches.

"He said they had to get all the witches. He went to the *pistoleros* who worked for Inocente, and he said they had to help him get the witches. He went to the Martinezes and said they had to help him get the witches. He went to some of the Sanchezes and said that they had to help too, or they would be the next to have someone killed. Don Martín told everyone to come down to the church and they took the body of that boy there. Everyone who was at the *velada,* the vigil, came, and there were a lot of other people there, too. They put the boy's body right there in front of the church, and everyone brought flowers. There were mountains of flowers for the boy and candles and incense, too.

"They all saw the boy. They didn't even have him wrapped up in a shroud. They left his clothes on him all covered with his blood, and they brought him up to the church. Martín Sandoval was furious. He was telling everyone that the witches would do this to everyone if they didn't stop them. Don Martín told everyone how many in his family had been witched, and then all the others started talking about how many they knew who had been witched. Everyone knew someone who those witches had sent into the earth. The witches had sent more people into the earth than those *pistoleros* ever had, and even they were afraid of the witches. Don Martín sat there all that day in the rain with the boy's body, crying with his mother and all the relatives and saying how foul the witches really were.

"That night there were a lot of the men down there, and there was a lot of *aguardiente*. They were all drinking, and they were all furious about the witches. There were a lot of witches then, but the really bad ones were not in town. They knew when to get out of there. Those men in the churchyard started to say who was a witch, and they went to their houses, but most of the people they said were witches fled. They split as fast as they could. Don Pedro's father took off, and so did Don Manuel Martinez and Eduardo Sanchez and Miguel Santos. The men went from house to house looking for the witches, but all of them had gone—the really bad ones at least, the really dangerous ones, that is."

I was taken aback by Doña María's straightforwardness. Had she been talking to Pedro and found out about my interest? Was there perhaps some other reason? Some connection between her and Pedro in the past? Had Pedro encouraged or coached her, I found myself wondering? Or was it Rubia? Assuming that what Doña María was saying was "true," at least for her, I tried to sort out the various "sides" in this affair and gave up. It was somewhat of a relief to just drive on and listen.

"They went to my uncle's house, which was just down the hill from our house, and we could hear them shouting, 'Where is that witch? Where is that murderous old witch!' They broke down the door, and my uncle was in there hiding. He hadn't left. They found him.

"They got him there in his house, and they tied him up, and they took him down to the plaza in front of the church where the boy was laid out. They all did horrible things to Martín. They hit him, and they burned his feet and his arms. He screamed he was going to kill them all, but they just kept on, all night. We could hear them out there all night with Uncle Martín. They did horrible things to him, but they didn't kill him. They kept him there where the boy's body was, and they beat him and burned him. They didn't want to kill him though, or another witch might get one of them.

"In the morning they got the cross out of the church, the one that they carry around the village on Good Friday, and they dug a hole for it there in the churchyard. They tied my uncle up to the cross, because they were going to take the boy off to the graveyard. They were going to bury him, but they left my uncle up there, tied up, bleeding, and burned. He was there all day while everyone buried the boy. No one dared to come out of their house, but you could hear my uncle screaming that they were all going to get it. The earth would consume them all, he was screaming. They would all be dead. Don Raul and Don Pedro would get them, but when they didn't, he was screaming that Raul and Pedro and Inocente would be consumed, too. He said they would all die there in the earth!

"They buried the boy, and all of them came back to the churchyard and they did more horrible things to my uncle. They threw things at him and cut him and told him that they would do the same to Don Raul, Don Inocente, and Don Pedro if they could find them. That was what a witch deserved, they said. They were going to get all the witches, they said, and they went down to the Cruz place down the hill. There was lots of *aguardiente*. Every once in a while some of them would come back up the hill and beat or throw more things at my uncle, and he was still furious. Finally, someone threw a big rock and smashed his head in.

"My aunt and her son went down in the darkness, took Uncle Martín down, and wrapped him up. They put him on a horse and took him to Quetzalan to bury him there. They couldn't bury him in San Martín; all those people would have dug up his grave and thrown him to the animals, or into the caves. They said they didn't want any more witches there in San Martín.

"When they got to Quetzalan they went to Padre Hector, the priest at the graveyard. He lived there. They asked if they could bury my uncle, and they explained that people in San Martín thought he was a witch and didn't want him buried there. Padre Hector asked if he was a witch, and they all said that he was not, but he was a witch just like the others. Padre Hector went to bless the body, and when he saw what had happened, he called the police and the military commander. They arrested my aunt and her son. They kept both of them there in the jail in Quetzalan for days until they told them what had really happened to Uncle Martín. Then they brought Don Pedro, Pedro's father, and all the others in.

"The army went over to San Martín and got everyone who was left there. The Cruzes and the Sandovals had left, and so had most everyone else in town. My father took all of us down to the coffee plantations. I heard this from my aunt. She was in jail with Don Pedro and the others for several days, and then they let her go, but they took Pedro off to Puebla, and some of the others, too. That was when it ended. Don Raul went down to Puebla with Don Pedro's mother, and Don Inocente didn't come back for a long time. José Sandoval left, and so did Manuel Cruz. The Cruzes had witches from Yohualichan. There weren't many of them left, either, after all the killing had stopped. No one wanted to be known as a witch after that. They were all afraid that they would get it the way my uncle did. Even after Inocente came back and Don Pedro's son returned, there were no more witches, not the way there were before."

"But there are still witches, and there are still witches who seek people's souls. What about them?" I asked. I was surprised by the old woman's vivid recollections. She must have forgotten all her discomforts while telling this gory tale. Mine were forgotten, too. I was dumbfounded.

"Well, they aren't the same," Doña María said. "They aren't killers. Some of them can steal a soul with an evil glance or send an evil wind, and some of them know how to do a lot of evil things, but they don't do it, at least not much anymore, not like before." She was silent for several moments. Finally, she said, "There are all kinds of witches. Why, you could even be one."

I was surprised. "No, I wouldn't do that kind of thing."

"Well, you could, though. I'll bet you know some pretty foul things to do if you got hot enough. You learned them from Rubia and that witch Inocente, I am sure."

Just as she said that, we came over the pass beyond Río Frío and began our descent into Mexico City. Doña María gasped. She had never seen anything like that vast sea of lights glowing before her. I wondered what she likened them to. One old Zapotec I had brought into the city this way thought that each light was a separate village and that there were millions of towns in the valley. Most of their villages had only one electric light apiece, installed by the Federal Electrical Commission.

We continued to talk about witches for a bit, but she was enthralled by the view of the city. On the way into town I dropped the Garcías off as close as I could to the area where they lived. Everyone put on their packs, even Linda, and off they walked into the darkness to the García house, lost among the millions of other shacks of Mexico's lost cities.

When I arrived home it was well after midnight. I unloaded my things from the car and, looking up, saw that the flame of my votive candle had gone out. I went up to my study and lit another before going to bed.

That night was the last time that I dreamed of Arcadio Cruz. It was a rather strange dream. I was standing before a huge, white surface like a painting with a rough, black chalked triangle inscribed within a circle at about eye level. There was a single blue horizontal line below the circle and the triangle was shaded in with a color like that of the dusty streets I so often walked on. In the center of the triangle was a hole, through which a single dark eye stared at me.

Slowly, from directly above the uppermost point of the triangle, a giant pendulum began to swing back and forth. The eye blinked each time it went by. I had never seen anything so abstract before in a dream. I watched the eye and the pendulum. Then I noticed someone standing next to me there. I turned. It was Arcadio Cruz, and he gave me a big *abrazo,* holding me so tight I thought I couldn't breathe. I was pleased to see him again, and it made me feel good. I could feel myself smiling. He had not changed at all. He was the man in the picture.

"Now you know," he told me. He took my hand, leading me into the picture through the hole where the eye was. We followed a well-paved path through green jungles of ferns and huge elephant ears and bright impatiens and morning glories. I followed him down to the possum's burrow again, and we saw the elderly marsupial that had sheltered us before in dreams.

She took us in, but this time there was no witch outside. Then I walked up the banks of a long stream with Arcadio to a raging waterfall. It was so loud that we could no longer speak. We stood there, and old Doña María came out of the mists, walking around the pool as if she didn't see us. Arcadio started to climb the falls, and I followed, but then I fell.

I think that he yelled to me, "Now you know!" before I woke up, and I did know. I knew who had witched him and also who had done the same to Rubia. It was nearly dawn, and though I was dead tired from the drive I knew that I would get no more sleep. I went up to the study and began to write down all that I had heard and all that I had done in San Martín.

I KNEW I had to talk to Inocente again. I had to know why. It would be many weeks before I would have another opportunity to visit the Sierra. I thought constantly, trying to make sense of all that I had heard and seen: the tales of witchcraft and murder and the fervent denials of involvement or responsibility. I knew who the witches were, and I knew the methods of murder they had used— most of them, anyway. Yet for all the murders, there was no one responsible for them.

I told no one of this for a long time. I certainly couldn't tell my academic colleagues. No one I knew would have been able to understand all this. I did not know what to make of it all then, and I still, even after all these years, do not know what it all means. I knew, though, I had to talk to old Inocente again.

Weeks later, when I finally saw that spritely, white-haired old man, I didn't know how to approach the topic of witchcraft. I went to see him on the pretense of asking about his tales, but after a few minutes he knew that I was there for more than that. My questions were vague and wandered over vast generalities about who was responsible for witchcraft. He did not seem to want to understand.

Finally, he asked me point-blank, "Well, what is it you came here for?"

"I wanted to know about Rubia," I blurted out. "Why did you do that to her?"

"Do what?" he asked in all innocence.

"You witched her. You brought the 'shadow of death' upon her, and she's your *comadre!* Maybe she was even your woman! She was a mother to Lucas, your son, and she's your sister in the 'path.' She's your closest friend in town!" I was furious with the old man.

"She had them all, all the people who needed her help, her dreams," he said matter-of-factly, not taking any notice of my anger. "They didn't come to me. I asked for justice. I did what they needed. I did nothing more. 'They' did not take her," he reminded me with a satisfied look.

"But she almost died."

"That would have been just."

"Just? Just? . . . like with Don Arcadio Cruz?" I was becoming even more furious.

Inocente was now shocked by my anger as much as he was by my mention of Arcadio Cruz. Or was it by my foolishness?

"I seek justice. That is what we do on this earth. Arcadio Cruz was a witch."

"Well, so are you."

"And you, too, perhaps one day, if not yet. We must all seek justice here on this earth. It is our mother, our father, the earth that grants us justice. We do nothing here without their permission. We are but fruits of this earth. We all return to our mother, our father, the earth. A witch is only a witch for one who does not understand the way of the Most Holy Earth."

"But you killed Arcadio and almost killed your *comadre!*"

"I did nothing but serve the Lords of the earth," Inocente said with such finality that there was nothing I could do but get up and leave.

It was the last I ever saw of the old man.

TRACING THE PATH
TO TALOCAN

THE MOUNTAINS SURROUNDING "SAN MARTÍN" and "Quetzalan" have always been a place of refuge for those escaping the power struggles and other problems of richer and more accessible areas of Mexico. Joining the Otomí, Totonac, and Tepehua who had come earlier, many of the Toltec ancestors of the Sanmartinos fled there when their empire collapsed sometime in the twelfth century. Later, other groups arrived escaping the Spanish Conquest and its aftermath. Today it is hard to imagine that the peoples of San Martín, eking out a living growing corn or coffee or practicing simple building trades in this marginal area, carry on the traditions of the builders of empires, mighty pyramids, and great cities.

These ancient pyramids, plazas, and sacred precincts built by their ancestors and relatives dwarfed those of the Western world in their time. Exacting tribute from an area almost the size of Europe, the Aztec Empire was held together at its core by massive pageants, architectural grandeur, great markets, psychological fear, and ideological intimidation, and, above all, by the rituals of human sacrifice. These were acted out in the precincts of the Templo Mayor near the center of what is now Mexico City. It was there that the hearts of captive warriors were offered to the sun and wailing infants were drowned for Tlaloc, Lord of the earth and underworld.

The priests who performed these bloody rituals were not just gruesome murderers but what we would also call the learned men of the empire: the astronomers, keepers of books of dreams, soothsayers, and wise men. In dream trances, often aided by hallucinatory drugs, they would travel through the underworld, seeking to know the will of their gods. They were shamans, diviners, and healers in a grand style, who cared for both their people and their gods. They were the ancestors of the tradition followed by Rubia and Inocente.

Led by the priests, the Aztecs, like many groups before them, "emerged" in the northern deserts from Chicomoztoc, the "Seven-Cave Place." According to their myths they were the last group of barbarians to come from there. As they migrated south in search of the prophesied site of the founding of their great city Tenochtitlan, the site of modern-day Mexico City, the Aztecs began to pick up the traits of civilization. The Toltecs, who had previously dominated the Valley of Mexico, were for the Aztecs the great builders of Mesoamerican civilization. The Aztecs claimed the Toltecs as their source of legitimacy and adopted them as ancestors through a deft rewriting of history and dynastic lineages.

Long before the Aztecs completed their journey, the Toltecs had already abandoned their great city of Tula, in the modern state of Hidalgo northeast of Mexico City. The famous Quetzalcoatl was their mythical god-king. He was an ascetic priest who opposed human sacrifice and a king who provided for his people. He brought them "corn of five colors," "cotton of five colors," precious stones and metals, cacao, and rich feathers that were valued more highly than gold. It was from him that the arts and writing came as well.

Defeated and defamed in his capital city by the wiles of the sorcerer Tezcatlipoca, "Mirror's Smoke," Quetzalcoatl and his people set out for the east through the Sierra de Puebla and arrived on the shores of the Gulf of Mexico near modern Veracruz. There Quetzalcoatl met his final end in a fiery conflagration and merged with Venus as the morning star, promising his people he would return. In this mythological drama, Quetzalcoatl—the good king and bringer of light—and Tezcatlipoca—the evil sorcerer and bringer of darkness—played out a theme of duality that is pervasive in Mesoamerica. The tradition of Rubia and Inocente carries with it the same dual nature: the capacity to cure and the capacity to kill.

The Toltecs, though, were not the first great civilization of Mesoamerica. The rich highland valleys of central Mexico had already seen a thousand years of developing civilization before them. By the time the Toltecs had arrived from the northern wastes, toward the end of Mexico's Classic Period (about A.D. 200–600), the great urban center of Teotihuacan had already flourished and was now dying.

This vast city, located north of present-day Mexico City, was a multilingual, multiethnic metropolis of over one hundred thousand and a thriving center for trade throughout Mesoamerica. After a long period of decline, it was partly sacked and burned sometime around 650, perhaps by the Toltecs or their Nahua kin.

The flower Rubia drew for me on the dirt floor of the hut to illustrate the form and shape of the underworld is ubiquitous among the ruins of Teotihuacan. Perhaps it was an icon that constantly reminded the diverse peoples in the great city of their relationship to the earth and Talocan. Images of Tlaloc, Lord of *Tlalocan,* were everywhere in Teotihuacan, and his cult dominated the city.

Deep beneath the Pyramid of the Sun at Teotihuacan, a cave was recently found by archaeologists that was obviously of crucial importance and perhaps in use long before the pyramid was built. Emergence from "The Cave" is a constant theme even in the art of the Olmec, Mesoamerica's first civilization, which long preceded Teotihuacan. Doris Heyden was the first to suggest that this cave was perhaps a "Chicomoztoc" like that of the Aztecs, the mythical point of origin of the peoples of Mesoamerica. Rubia also talked a lot about a cave that was the "true heart," the true center of the underworld. This place, she said, was entered through a cave under the "Central Plaza" of the gods' city at the center of the underworld. Perhaps the cave underneath the Pyramid of the Sun was the entry to that same sacred place.

No one knows who built Teotihuacan, or who the Olmecs really were, and as we go further back in time the search for the ultimate originators of the worship of the earth and sky becomes gradually lost. We are finally left with archaeological dating of bits of bones, corn, potsherds, charcoal, and the smoke on the ceilings of those sacred caves.

AFTER THE SPANISH Conquest in the early sixteenth century, most of what we know about the history and traditions of pre-Columbian peoples was written down by Spanish friars, who interviewed only a handful of the 20 percent of the native population that survived the holocaust of the Conquest. Most of these accounts were marred by mistranslations and the pervading ideas of Christian "Truth," along with the habitual historical revisionism of the Aztecs themselves. None of the Aztec dream books, astrological tracts, or divinatories remained, and nearly all the Aztec priests and political and military leaders had perished or fled. The search for the origins of Inocente and Rubia's tradition thus involves a complicated decoding of scanty archaeological, linguistic, and mythological data. When this is combined with the written texts, history, reality, horror, and the worlds of dreams, trances, and revelations often merge.

The military and political conquest of the Aztec Empire by the Spaniards took only a few years, but the spiritual conquest of its people and villages, especially in mountain refuges, was not so rapid. When the first twelve Franciscans arrived in Veracruz and walked to Mexico City in imitation of the twelve apostles, they made thousands of converts, baptizing the natives of the New World by the millions, according to their own estimates. At first, native enthusiasm for this new kingdom of Christendom was boundless. Converts helped tear down the temples, quickly building massive cathedrals and schools in their place.

By the latter half of the sixteenth century, however, it became clear that traditional Aztec ways could not be extinguished as easily as their temples had been torn down, their priests eliminated, and their books burned. The natives of this New World, though they worshiped the gods, saints, and virgins of the friars with great passion, still kept the old with the new. Revelations of native "superstition" and "idolatry," often obtained through torture by the second and third waves of Catholic priests, and rebellions led by messianic leaders such as Juan Ocelotl in the Sierra de Puebla soon showed civil and religious authorities that they had far to go to eliminate native beliefs.

Today, after four hundred years, the work of the friars has resulted in a public religion that supports a civil and Catholic hierarchy; it is true that the worship of the "Sky God," his Son, and the saints has replaced the old ideas of the role of sacrificed human blood in maintaining the flow of the universe. But beneath this is a private, household religion, largely unknown to outsiders. The Nahua Indians still pray to the Most Holy Earth, Talocan. This is not syncretism or a mixture—the two systems exist side by side. Rubia was at once a good Catholic and a servant of the Lords of the Earth.

In recent discoveries among the Nahua, there is more, however, than a question of the survival of ancient beliefs. Once the turmoil of the Conquest had settled down and the survivors had adjusted to the new order, peace returned. The villagers re-created their traditional way of life by planting and harvesting corn, soaking it in lime, grinding it, and making it up into tortillas to wrap around beans and sauces much as their ancestors had done.

Trouble soon came again, however. First it was from the French, who marched through the Sierra on their way to defend the puppet emperor Maximilian in the 1860s. Then came shock waves, mostly from the north, emanating outward from the rapid economic development of the United States and Europe in the late nineteenth century. Seeing the potential for cash crops of coffee, the *caciques* on the east coast of Mexico saw a lucrative market in New Orleans that had been controlled up to that point by Brazilians. As exports increased, the planting of coffee spread up into the mountain areas of Mexico, and in the success of the early days, these moguls were given a reverence by the local peoples similar to that accorded the old mythical god-kings. These were the *patrones,* the lords, to whom goods were offered and from whom sustenance could be expected.

The coffee boom lasted into the twentieth century, but because it was tied into an international market, local producers eventually lost control of their economic fate. The introduction of a cash crop ultimately meant the disruption of the traditional economy, while the consequent social disruption resulted in the rise of new families and lineages and the fall of previously important ones. Along with these conflicts and rivalries came the intensification of revolutionary pressures for villagers to become part of the national Mexican culture. Using the ancient belief system, not only because it was effective, but because it lay outside the national law, villagers reacted in their own way to these pressures. The result in San Martín was the War of Witches where, if villagers' accounts are correct, well over a hundred people died.

This war ended in a tacit agreement among the villagers never to use those methods again. While mestizos in the nearby urban areas could regard San Martín as "full of witches" in a vague sense fifty years after the event, it was possible for the villagers to deny the war ever happened. In short, there was a process going on that was similar to the rewriting of history in the old Aztec style of creating "order out of chaos." It was only because of my involvement on a personal level with the tradition, language, and ways of the Sanmartinos that I was able to discover this before Rubia and her fellow survivors died about ten years ago.

Though three million Nahuas continue to live their lives in insular isolation throughout Mexico, they still do not openly discuss their religion, despite today's rather relaxed political and economic situation. They feel these beliefs are unimportant to outsiders, but when asked in the right way, in their own language, their eyes will brighten, and they may reply, if they are not too afraid, "*Ticmati ipan in talocan:* Ah, you know the underworld."

GLOSSARY

A Note on the Pronunciation of Aztec Terms

The orthography used here is based on an orthography developed for Classic Aztec by Spanish friars in the sixteenth century; it was based on the pronunciation of sixteenth-century Spanish. The vowels generally follow those of modern Spanish, and differences in length are not distinguished but do exist. The *j* is used for the glottal occlusive, which sounds more like an *h* in English. The *hu* and *uh* combinations are pronounced as our *w*. The *qu* combination before *a* is pronounced as in "quiet" but as a *k* elsewhere. The *x* is pronounced like the English *sh,* and the combination of *tl* is a single sound, as in "kettle."

abrazo   A hug given as greeting in Latin countries.

Acihuat   The "Water Woman," the Lady of the Eastern Waters of the underworld, who usually resides in the House of Women in the West.

aguacil   Literally, "executioner," but generally a post in the civil hierarchy of most towns equivalent to a constable.

aguardiente   A potent distilled alcoholic beverage widely used in the Sierra.

ahuane   One of the supernaturals of Talocan, literally, "water one." *Ahuane* are the resident deities of the waters and are found in every pool and stream of the Sierra.

ajmotocnihuan   Literally, "those who are not our brothers." A term referring to all the supernaturals considered to be the servants of the Lords of Talocan.

Alas   A very potent brand of cigarette used in the Sierra.

alpixque   Some of the supernaturals of Talocan, literally, "the water keepers," who release the waters of streams, waterfalls, and springs.

Apan   Literally, the "Water Place." Also the Great Sea of the East of the underworld.

atole   A corn gruel, often flavored with sugar or chile.

Atotonican   Literally, the "Place of Boiling Waters," but also the source of heat in the South of the underworld, home to the Colohuetzin, or earth monster.

autoridades   The town or village officials.

bigote   From Spanish, a short mustache.

cacique   A local political strongman.

cafetal   A coffee garden.

calzones   Literally, "underwear," but generally referring to the white poplin wraparound pants worn by peasants throughout Mexico.

cazuela   An open bowl-like Mexican ceramic cooking pot.

Chicomoztoc   The "Seven-Cave Place," the mythical point of origin for the peoples of Mesoamerica.

chilpotzontli   A sauce made of chilpoctli chiles with roasted tomato, garlic, and onion, usually flavored with a bit of allspice in the Sierra.

Colohuetzin   The earth monster considered the Lord of the South of Talocan.

comadre/compadre   The godparent, or sponsor of a ritual event for someone, who then becomes the equivalent of kin. There are special obligations involved in the relationship.

comal   A griddle for toasting tortillas and other foods.

copal   Pitch incense.

copitas   Little glasses, or the drinks of fiery alcohol served in them.

curandera/curandero   Native curer; a practitioner of traditional medicine.

ecahuil   Literally, the "shadow." A term used to refer to the cool or dark side of a *tonal* that is shared with the *nagual*.

Ejecacihuat   The "Wind Woman," the Lady of the Winds of the North of the underworld, who usually resides in the House of Women in the West.

Ejecatan   The "Cave of the Winds" in the North of Talocan.

epazote   A slightly bitter herb referred to in English as "pig's root" and widely used in Mexico for its culinary and medicinal properties.

gorditas   Corn dough wrapped around a savory paste of beans or pork cracklings. They are toasted on a griddle, or *comal.*

Ilhuicac   The sky, a general name in Nahua for one of the three realms of the supernatural. The sky is the focus of the public cults of the saints, virgins, and Jesucristo.

Ipalnemoani   A concept of an ultimate diety, which is often glossed as "He who gives us life." First used in Classic Aztec prayers, it is still in use today.

juez   Judge.

kiyauhtiomej   Some of the supernaturals of Talocan, literally, "the lightning ones." They can live anywhere but generally reside in the Cave of the Winds.

Llorona   The "Weeping Woman" of Mexican folklore, usually equated with the Acihuat, "the Water Woman," who lurks around the wells and streams seeking to capture men unfaithful to their wives.

mapache   An Aztec term for a raccoon borrowed into Mexican Spanish.

mayordomo   The individual in charge of a particular event, such as a procession or saint's festival in the official religious hierarchy.

metate   A grinding stone.

mictiani   Some of the supernaturals of Talocan, literally, "the ones who bring Death." They are considered by villagers to be eaters of human flesh.

milpa   A traditional cornfield.

Miquitalan   Literally, "earth of the dead," or cemetery, but also the Land of the Dead in the North of Talocan.

mole   A term borrowed from Aztec meaning "sauce." Today, it generally refers to a rich chile sauce with chocolate typical of Puebla. It is usually served at festivals or on special occasions.

nagual   One of the three aspects of the soul, equated with an individual's animal alter ego.

nagualli   A witch or transforming shaman with multiple *naguals* capable of both good and evil.

Nahua   A general ethnic term referring to all of the peoples speaking Modern Aztec dialects.

Nahuat   The dialect of Modern Aztec spoken in the Sierra de Puebla around San Martín.

naoalli   A sixteenth-century spelling of *nagualli* from Classic Aztec.

ocote   Fatwood, a resinous wood used for torches and for lighting fires.

Olmecs   The people generally considered to be the originators of the earliest Mesoamerican high civilization, which developed on the coast of Veracruz.

Otomí   An indigenous group inhabiting the states of Mexico and Hidalgo in the central highlands of Mexico. It is not known for certain when they arrived in the Sierra de Puebla.

petate   A large woven reed mat used for sleeping and sitting upon.

Quetzalcoatl   The feathered serpent deity and the god-king of the Toltecs; one of the central cultural heroes of Mesoamerica. Some perceived Cortez as the returning Quetzalcoatl.

refino   A potent type of *aguardiente,* cane alcohol, used in the Sierra de Puebla.

susto   A Spanish term for magical fright, or soul loss.

Taloc   A term used guardedly in the Sierra that refers to the Lord, or embodiment, of Talocan. All the Lords and Ladies of the underworld are aspects of this chief Lord, who lived in or was Talocan's center, or "heart."

Talocan   The underworld of the ancestors of San Martín, referred to in Spanish as both the "Most Holy Earth" and the "inferno."

talocanca   Some of the supernaturals of Talocan, literally, "the ones from Talocan," who are servants of the Lords of the underworld.

Talticpac   The surface of the earth, where human beings and the natural world coexist between the two realms of the supernatural: the sky, Ilhuicac, and the underworld, Talocan.

tatoani   Literally, "he who says something." The speaker, leader, or lord of a group of people.

tecuani   Literally, a "people eater"; often used to refer to jaguars.

Teotihuacan The city of the pyramids outside Mexico City, which, at its height, dominated Mexico's Classic Period (about A.D. 200–750).

tepalcates Pre-Columbian potsherds; a general term for broken pottery.

Tepehua A group of indigenous people living at the northern edges of the Sierra de Puebla. No one is certain when they came.

tepehuane Some of the supernaturals of Talocan, literally, "the hill people," who are found in the "savage" part of the world outside the villages. They harvest and cut trees, hunt animals, and capture people who are "not living well."

tepeyolomej Some of the supernaturals of Talocan, literally, "the hill heart ones," who reside in caves and mountain shrines and embody the hills.

Tezcatlipoca "Mirror's Smoke," the sorcerer deity of the Aztec world, who fought with Quetzalcoatl and defeated him.

tlacuache Opossum (an Aztec term incorporated into Mexican Spanish).

Tlaloc Classic Aztec god of earth and water, the Lord of Tlalocan.

Tlalocan The Classic Aztec term for the underworld and the equivalent of Talocan.

Toltecs A people who developed a civilization in central Mexico in the eleventh to thirteenth centuries. Their capital was Tula, Hidalgo. The Toltecs were probably the ancestors of the people of San Martín.

tonal One of the three aspects of the soul, equated with the spark of life, fate, or luck of an individual. It is this aspect of the soul that travels in dreams.

Tonallan Literally, the "Place of the Sun," the western edge of Talocan where the House of Women is found.

Totonac   An indigenous group inhabiting the Sierra de Puebla and much of the state of Veracruz. No one is certain when they arrived or where they came from.

velada   A Spanish term for a funeral vigil.

yolixpa   A strong, sweet, greenish alcoholic beverage made from *aquardiente* and infused with herbs. It is not unlike Chartreuse.

yollo   An aspect of the soul that is equated with the heart. This is the internal life force that gives the body movement and life.

ACKNOWLEDGMENTS

PETER SHOTWELL, AN OLD FRIEND AND A PROFESSIONAL writer and editor based in China and Japan, first convinced me to tell this tale at the Yak Hotel in Lhasa, Tibet. We had traveled together from Chengdu, the capital of Szechuan province, by horse, truck, jeep, and bus across the high plateau of Qinghai before we finally made it to Lhasa. I had planned to work on a rather different and much more academic book, but Chinese authorities seized the research materials I had brought with me to China—things written in strange languages like Spanish and Aztec, of course, must be seditious materials. Shotwell, along with Edwina Williams, Larry Sullivan, and an ever-increasing audience of trekkers, travelers, tourists, and pilgrims, listened to the first version of this tale over a period of two nights in Lhasa. Edwina, as a good anthropologist, recorded it. Shotwell and I then made an outline while visiting remote Bon-po monasteries in the Tibetan highlands. We made a final plan for this book as we traveled out of Tibet into Yunnan province. On the way out of China I managed to stop in Japan, where Shotwell and I worked out the first chapters at the offices of Ishi Press. It was there that I convinced him to come down to my home on Water Island in the U.S. Virgin Islands, where we finished a first draft. Later, in New York, we both worked in tandem, writing and editing the story together. Though there are many people who took a part in making this book, its final shape is largely due to Peter Shotwell.

There are many others, though, who must be acknowledged for having played a part in the nearly twenty years of research in Mexico on which this book is based. First of all, my friends, colleagues, and students at the Instituto de Investigaciones Antropológicas at the National University of Mexico (UNAM), the National Institute and the National School of Anthropology and History (INAH and ENAH), and the National Indian Institute (INI), as well as hundreds of friends in the remote regions of Mexico, are owed my deepest gratitude. The people of remote rural villages were my best teachers. Among my colleagues in Mexico who especially influenced this work were Doris Heyden, the nurturing mother of generations of anthropologists, and my late teachers Dr. Karl Heidt, Fernando Horcasitas, Don Ignacio Bernal, Thelma D. Sullivan, and Dr. Paul Kirchoff. The many anthropologists, historians, economists, and sociologists interested in Mexican religions, Yolotl Gonzalez Torres, Elio Masferrer Kan, Johanna Broda, B. Dhalgren, Alfredo Lopez Austin, Mercedes Olivera, Neomi Quezada, MaEugenia Sanchez, Eduardo Alemeda, and many, many others are owed a great debt of gratitude. Jaimie Litvak King, the late Guillermo Bonfils, Don Antonio Pompa y Pompa, Enrique Meyer, Luis Vargas, Maricarmen

Sera Puche, Miguel Leon-Portilla, and many others provided both institutional support and encouragement. This work over the years was supported by grants from the National Endowment for the Humanities, the American Philosophical Society, the National University of Mexico, and the Universidad de las Americas.

Among my friends and colleagues here in the United States, Dennis and Barbara Tedlock, Peter and Jill Furst, B. J. Price, B. J. Isbell, Gary Gossen, David Carrasco, Tony Avini, Willard Gingerich, Elizabeth Boone, Evelyn Rattray, Duncan Earle, John Pohl, Richard Haily, Ken Hirth, Dave Grove, and Bill Sanders, as well as many others, have encouraged and influenced this book. Pedro Lujan, Edwina Williams, Peter Wolfe, Michael Knab, Mrs. E. Olson, Dexter Kelly, Kathy Goss, Taj Jackson, Janine Pommy Vega, Shelton P. Applegate, G. A. Donovan, and others all commented on the manuscript. Susan Long did an especially fine job on the final edit of this book. Marial Thomson and Claire Ritter provided places to stay while we finished the book, and the help of Anne Walker and Claire's staff at Chantik was invaluable. Richard Bozulich, along with Gene Andrews and the staff at Andrews Building Corporation, gave highly appreciated help and support to Peter. The hospitality of Evelyn Rattray will also not be forgotten. There is also one angel who must be mentioned: Merle Ogle, Doris Heyden's sister, without whose help I probably could not have finished. Rick Balkin, agent extraordinaire, provided the present title and has made substantial editorial comments. Chefs Alain Sailhac, Jacques Pepin, Martin Schaub, and Robert Shapiro at the French Culinary Institute helped me find the time to finish work on this piece. In the U.S. Virgin Islands, the people of Mafolie Foods and Cafe Normandie, especially George Johnson, will always be appreciated. Editorial comments by John Loudon, Karen Levine, and our production editor, Luann Rouff, at Harper San Francisco have also substantially influenced this book.

Finally, it is the people of the village I have chosen to call San Martín, especially my teachers whom I have called Rubia and Inocente, who must be thanked for their warmth, trust, hospitality, and kindness. The final form of this book may not satisfy all those who know this material, and I must take full responsibility for the devices I have used in forging a story out of this material. My primary concern was to write narrative anthropology forming a complete, concise, compelling narrative that would carry the load of years of experience, yet remain readable. I can only hope that this book conveys some of the essence of the discovery, adventure, and learning of twenty years of field work.

Timothy J. Knab

DECEMBER 25, 1994
CUERNAVACA, MORELOS
MEXICO

Printed in the United States
44220LVS00002B/87